Mary Thorn Carpenter

In Cairo and Jerusalem

An Eastern Note-Book

Mary Thorn Carpenter

In Cairo and Jerusalem
An Eastern Note-Book

ISBN/EAN: 9783743417151

Manufactured in Europe, USA, Canada, Australia, Japa

Cover: Foto ©Andreas Hilbeck / pixelio.de

Manufactured and distributed by brebook publishing software (www.brebook.com)

Mary Thorn Carpenter

In Cairo and Jerusalem

IN CAIRO AND JERUSALEM

AN EASTERN NOTE-BOOK

BY

MARY THORN CARPENTER

AUTHOR OF "A GIRL'S WINTER IN INDIA"

With Illustrations

NEW YORK
ANSON D. F. RANDOLPH AND COMPANY
(INCORPORATED)
182 FIFTH AVENUE

To a sweet Little Girl,

THAT THESE PAGES MAY REVEAL TO HER SOMETHING OF THE
CHARM OF A FAR COUNTRIE WHICH THE MAGICIAN
TIME WILL DISSOLVE BEFORE HER BABY
EYES SHALL GROW TO GRASP IT.

LITTLE REST, MILLBROOK,
    NEW YORK, 1894.

CONTENTS.

A CHRONICLE OF CAIRO.

The New Hotel. — The Season's Pleasures. — Sylphs or Saïs. — Cairo at Dinner. — The Old Quarters and the New Streets. — In the Mousky. — Egypt's Latest Master, Ismail Pasha 1

GIZEH.

Dividing the Day. — On Donkeys to Gizeh. — The Approach to the Museum. — Petrie the Explorer. — An Egyptian Lady's "Idlesse."— The Royalties. — Scarabs. — Profits in Antiques. — The Court of the Dead. — Pharaoh in his Mummy-Case. — The Best Preserved of the Mummies 19

FROM A CAIRO JOURNAL.

The Bazaars. — Spices from Araby. — The Mosques. — Old Tooloon. — A Mohammedan Chapel. — The Hidden Jewels of the Shrine. — Its Visitors. — The Veiled Worshippers 50

IN THE FAYÛM.

                                                         PAGE

An Oasis in Sahara. — By Goods Train to Medinet-el-Fayûm. — A Barrack in the Desert. — The Mudir and his People. — First Acquaintance with a Native Inn. — Amateur Antiquarians. — Crocodilopolis the Ancient. — A Fallen Obelisk 62

A DAY'S EXCURSION TO HAWARA.

Native Donkey-Boys. — Egypt's Fertile Soil. — On the Edge of the Desert. — Lake Mœris. — Joseph's Problem. — The Labyrinthine Wonders. — Birket-el-Kurûn, or the Lake of the Horns. — A Sunset under the Libyan Hills. — A Circus in the Fayûm. — Saint Roubé's Orisons 85

THE CAIRO OF THE MOSLEMS.

The University of El Azhar. — A New and Original Campus. — College Lodgings. — The Wiseacres of Egypt. — The Curriculum. — A Hard-Won Purchase. — The Muristan. — Mohammed Ali 101

A SHEIK'S HOUSE.

Lazarus at the Gate. — A Peacock Room. — The State Band-Box. — An Oriental Room. — A Telephone. — The Mohammedan Paradise. — " In Shallah " . . . 115

WITH COOK AT SAKKARA.

A Sheik of Travellers. — Old Nilus. — The Sail on the River. — Fighting for Donkeys. — The Start from Sakkara. — Mariette Bey's House. — Luncheon. — The Serapeum. — Scampering back to the "Queen Hatasu" 129

A DAY WITH THE COPTS.

A Friend from the Mission. — Corner Scenes. — A Coptic House. — The Life of the Copts. — Matrimony and its Coronation. — The Patriarch of All the Copts. — The Visit Returned by Proxy 147

IN A COPTIC CATHEDRAL.

A Morning Walk. — Unfamiliar Services. — Aspects of the Congregation. — " Suffer the Little Children." — An Altar Boy and his Saints. — Two Years ago in the Cathedral 163

JAFFA TO JERUSALEM.

Good-by to Alexandria. — A Turkish Steamer. — Jaffa. — The Landing. — A Ticket for Jerusalem. — Investment in Shares of the Railway. — Lydda. — " Look! how nice! from here is Jerusalem!" 173

THE NEW JERUSALEM.

                                                                PAGE

Outside the Walls. — A Dull Town. — The Suburbs. — Russian Monks. — Easter Pilgrims. — Monastic Properties and Great Religious Houses. — Materials of Stone 188

SOME JEWISH COLONIES.

The Jews. — The German Colony. — Montefiore Alms-Houses. — The Jaffa District. — "Yawash" a Good Motto. — Fair Palestine 198

THE BOX COLONY.

Last Days in Jerusalem. — Sir Balaam in Palestine. — A Cheerless Colony. — The Box Colony. — Upside-down Colonization. — Laborers in Abraham's Vineyard. — An English College at Goath. — "The King's Winepress." — A Stranger in a Strange Land 209

LIST OF ILLUSTRATIONS.

	PAGE
A Fayûm Madonna	*Frontispiece*
On the Nile	49
Some Fellâhîn Women	50
An Egyptian Orchestra	58
Mosque of Kait Bey	74
A Bazaar by the Bahr Yusuf	78
Some Old Houses, Medinet	79
A Medinet Beauty	87
A Fellah Boy	88
A Fellâhîn Repast	101
The Citadel	113
A School near the Mosque	115
Shepheard's Hotel	129
A Scribe and a Coptic's Correspondent	147
At a Street Corner	149
Railroad Station at Jerusalem	185
A Street in Jerusalem	191

IN CAIRO AND JERUSALEM.

A CHRONICLE OF CAIRO.

TEA and toast were being served on the terrace of the New Hotel, when a dusty arabiyeh — the victoria of Cairo, drawn by two gaunt horses — drew up before the front entrance, and we were rushed through rows of small tea-tables and hooded chairs, past the bright awnings, which shaded the John Bull section of men and maidens, in riding costume, who were easily distinguishable, even at half a glance, from the French and Russians flowering forth in colors like a rose-garden. The occupants of the draped and much-bedecked piazza seemed fain to keep clear of us and our dust; the tourist who arrives tired and travel-stained from Ismaïlia generally preferring rather to see than to be seen. On this occasion only, he merely sniffs the refreshing tea-fumes, and is rapidly conducted towards the office, where he is glad to follow his boxes to any number left unoccupied in the crowded hotel. "It is the season," explains the manager, as he hands the servant a key which fits a door on the third floor, promising at the same time to move you down at the first vacancy, — a promise which would be unnecessary, if there was only a lift to get you up. Two high bedsteads shrouded in white mosquito netting make an unfavorable first impression of your apartment. This impression was dissipated, however, by an Arab boy, who appeared at our door after several attempts to follow out the directions posted on the side wall, to "press the electric button" to summon the maid. Each effort resulted in bringing the dusky servant, who was as many times dismissed, until finally I commanded him to bring the chambermaid, to which he meekly replied, "Madam, I am she," and produced a queer old amphora of fresh water which might have belonged to Pharaoh's daughter; and if we took the plagues of Egypt along with its other antiquities, no one could object to that.

The New Hotel, an unsentimental-looking pile, stands out with its Moorish pretensions opposite a well-shaded garden in the Place Ezbekīyeh. The greenery all about the terrace shows foliage which shadows the grass and keeps it beautifully green. From this wide veranda, carpeted with gay Turkish rugs, are hung red and blue draperies of white canvas, with designs of stars and crescents sewed on them by the artisans of the Tunis bazaar to suit the taste of the Oriental customer.

The world of Cairo not only, but the entire East, passes by the New Hotel in a never-ending panoramic procession. At the entrance, dragomen of all nationalities, with all colors of Eastern turbans, and all alike in brightly-braided jackets, offer their services to the new-comers in clamorous phrases of self-praise, or, when invention fails in this line, chatter and laugh among themselves like so many magpies. I am at my wit's end sometimes in a vain mental search for a country which will fit their curious clothes and unfamiliar contours. Greeks, Copts, Abyssinians with soft gazelle eyes, Nubians and Algerians dressed in short or long garments with bare or draped arms, propose their services as guides, dragomen, or conductors to the Cairene sights. A cavass of one of the different consulates, richly dressed in silver and gold embroidered stuffs, with flashing cimeter at his side, flourishes a long cane with a golden point, which he uses effectually while proudly pushing aside the throng of foot passengers who are constantly moving past the entrance to the hotel, where the servant awaits his master. In the throng a European dress is sometimes seen, but is drowned in the overflow of brilliantly draped Orientals of all races. Merchants, with ostrich plumes and antiquities more or less authentic,—

native bottles, and scarabs or rugs and spears from the Soudan,— saunter through this busiest of thoroughfares. Women enveloped in a long drapery, the face hidden under a veil, and only showing their feet, shod in satin slippers of a striking color, force their way past an Arab trotting along on his meek-looking donkey with the utmost carelessness, as calm as glass in contrast to the conscious embarrassment of a European, who, in the same position, always looks as if he were doing something ridiculous. Then the freshly imported closed broughams of the harem dash by, dividing the shining sea of color, which rolls back as the saïs gracefully clear the way, running swiftly a few yards in advance of the superb horses.

The saïs are the most sylph-like beings imaginable; scarcely touching the ground, they can run for hours without tiring, — nothing fatigues them; their costume is delicious, a little theatrical perhaps, but not too strange or bright under the burning Eastern sunshine. A vest richly decorated and embroidered in gold arabesques, a wide silk sash with ends floating far in the wind, and a pair of loose, gauzy sleeves immaculately white, falling to the waist, meet a short skirt of the same material, and make a costume so delicate and light, and with so little friction in it, that it is no more an impediment to rapid motion than a soft white cloud would be if it could be utilized for like purposes on *terra firma*. It is to the Mamelukes that Cairo owes the saïs. Each of these cavaliers was accompanied by a runner, who carried his weapons, adroitly recovering them, should they fall during a combat, gliding in and out of the fray, doing all the mischief possible to the enemy by cutting their saddle-bands and exasperating the horses with well-delivered and demoralizing sword-cuts. But the race is dying out; the saïs is *passé* at thirty, and at forty has weakness of the lungs, to which he generally succumbs. In Egypt, nature demands that men should be lotus-eaters, not sylphs of perpetual motion.

One of the first things that attracted our attention among the sights of the Place Ezbekīyeh was a string of blue-robed women marching bare-footed in couples, preceded by a company of Arabs with woful countenances, who sang a funeral dirge in a nasal, monotonous chant, the measure and rhythm of which changed every now and again, as the earnestness deepened. The men were Muezzins, or hired mourners, who are paid by the hour to recite the Korân on such occasions, and we soon perceived that it was a funeral procession. The corpse, wrapped in a coarse cashmere shawl, was laid on a bier head foremost, a board wrapped in silks at each end, on which was pinned the golden jewelry worn by the poor woman, who had died that morning. The company also included women hired to howl, and beat their breasts at the Mohammedan Cemetery under the Mokattam hills, about a mile from the city, where the sandy soil is catacombed with graves in every direction, and there the dead are laid to rest with their faces turned towards Mecca. Here the wailing and lamenting is renewed every Thursday and Friday following, until forty days have elapsed, and then a large stone is rolled on the new grave to accommodate the angel who will surely come to instruct the faithful on the answers they are to give on the Catechismal Day of Judgment.

At the mystic hour of sunset, a little Arabian fairy darts out apparently from the feathery tufts which fringe and tangle the shady paths of the Ezbekīyeh garden. This little woodland elf, scarcely less graceful than the pliant shrubbery and the lovely, bright, flying things, is like nothing else in Cairo. Clinging like a delicate tendril to the iron rail about the terrace, where the tourists are taking their tea, she glances wistfully from one to another; then her pretty pink draperies and long black braids catch some one's eyes, and she begins a low, cooing chant, "Tirili, Tirili, Tirili," — a weird warble which she produces from her vocal chords by merely pressing her finger-tips on the throat, as if playing a stringed lute. Presently she falls into a phantom dance, executed with wild pirouettes, always in time to the elfish music.

At half after seven all Cairo dines, and the hungry tourist turns gratefully to the flesh-pots of Egypt, when they are served at a well appointed *table d'hôte*, quite in keeping with semi-Europeanized Cairo. The dinner is very beautiful, brightened with the evening dresses of scores of Continental belles seated at two long tables, conversing gayly with the English officers from the Citadel, or striving to put at ease a native Egyptian wearing an orthodox scarlet fez, who is apparently listening with deep attention to his fair companion while mentally deciding whether to use his fingers or his fork to the *champignons à la crème* handed him by the waiter. The oddest part of the scene is the sprinkling of red head-gear up and down the dining-room, which belongs to every shade of Eastern complexion, — Copts, Turks, and even Jews, the latter having returned in large numbers to the land of Goshen, this time for the "season" only, when they dwell in beautiful villas and possess hotels and valuable corner lots in their ancient House of Bondage.

Baedeker solves the sight-seeing problem for every new tourist who confides his stay in Cairo to the guidance and rules contained in his little red book. By carefully following out the prescribed disposition of twelve working hours, the principal attractions of Cairo may be seen in six days, according to the guide-book. Having never tried this method of doing Cairo, I cannot dispute the fact, but can only say that indefatigable perseverance during two visits of several weeks' duration has failed to make an impression on the bazaars alone; and without going outside of the Place Ezbekīyeh, a month's study would hardly suffice to comprehend its endless street-scenes, which have been described a thousand times, but defy description.

The most important street in Cairo is undoubtedly the Mousky, belonging to the old French quarter; narrow, and bordered with tall houses, with all sorts of balconies suspended in seeming insecurity from their shaky surroundings. The guides call it the Cairene "Rue de Rivoli." Doubtless that famous avenue had once upon a time just as humble a beginning; but when I first saw the narrow, dingy Mousky, it was indeed difficult to believe it. Up and down the street are open booths, jutting out a little over the pavement, all the more to allure the shoppers and literally make them walk over the merchandise spread out under their feet, and above their heads. A calm almost religious presides over the little shopkeepers' transactions. The importunate demands of the Parisian merchants to buy, the embarrassing discussion regarding the merits of the bargain counter in our modern shops, is entirely absent, and silence reigns over the beautiful Eastern fabrics and embroideries of the Mousky; although if ever merchants should stand excused for vaunting their goods, it is these old Persians. Even the old system of bargaining is succeeded by a placard at the entrance of every important shop, announcing "Prix fixe,"—an innovation which is rather strictly carried out in practice, but entirely circumvented in principle by the substantial backsheesh given by the merchant to an initiated customer.

At an afternoon tea a well-known member of the French nobility, wintering in Cairo, showed us an exquisite unset turquoise embedded in red wax on a piece of bamboo, in order to display its beauty quite unadorned. To my amazement the noble dame, with her distinguished air and manners, confessed, without a trace of humiliation, that she had received the stone that morning as backsheesh from the hands of a popular Persian jeweller in the Place Ezbekīyeh, and I better understood that Nature's touch which makes us all akin is the golden one. What is the difference between a piastre and a precious stone, although one satisfies a duchess and the other a donkey boy; it is all equal except in the mind of man.

The Mousky is very unlike the native parts of the city, — still it is not Eastern, nor yet modern: tall houses with overhanging cornices jutting far out over the street shade the narrow avenue; civilization has penetrated these semi-Europeanized shops in some slight degree, and one finds that waxen figures clad in Saxon clothes from Regent Street have superseded the Oriental draperies in the shop windows, and these flaxen-haired gentlemen are gazed at as curiously by the Oriental throng as a full-fledged Madame Tussaud's wax-work exhibition would be in London, could the positions be reversed; but, luckily, the Levantines alter the cut of their coats, as well as the methods of their speech, very gradually. Sewing-machines and pianos are found in the Mousky, but rarely Koráns and turbans, which makes one regret and applaud twenty times within the hour.

The magnificent white donkeys with saddles of red morocco or yellow velvet, and bridles tinkling with rows of silver chains reaching nearly to the ground, are, however, as barbarous as one could desire; and so are the long low trucks drawn by oxen, bringing goods from the caravansaries or Khâns to the shops, where it is an overpowering temptation to linger among the fascinating silver stuffs, gold embroideries, and webby gauzes; but the desire to push on to more wonderful sights is even more tempting.

From our saddle perch we pass in review all the brilliant tissues of silver thread and silken stripes, which are the turbans of the dragoman, and gallop through the confusion of men, women, and children, blind beggars, camels, and humble asses with shabby harness mended with bits of string. "Yallah, Yallah!" calls the donkey boy, encouraging his beast at the same time with blows from a small stick. The patient animal has slackened his speed, and a carriage drawn by two superb horses is impeded in its rapid progress by a string of camels, who can literally be described as "stopping the way." "Yallah, go on!" calls the little Arab, louder and more determined than before; and by a miracle we circle both obstacles, and in a moment more arrive at the end of the Mousky, so dazzled by all that has passed that we dismount and take breath. The faith and confidence of the donkey boy in his Prophet alone has prevented our being crushed and crumbled into fragments in the seething caldron of Eastern humanity.

New Cairo has been created out of the *débris* of the old city; all about the ancient quarter are the tumbling remains of palaces, mosques, and once great and sumptuous houses. The modern Cairenes rarely repair or rebuild their beautiful monuments, which were never remarkable for solidity, and were frequently erected in haste with the material nearest at hand; for it seems far better to the Eastern mind to abandon the most exquisite ruin, and utilize the ornaments or stone-work in the construction of a new building. Even then, provided the chiselled bronzes and brilliant arabesques are beautiful to look upon, the Oriental cares little if the fragile construction sways with the wind, or crumbles in the atmospheric dampness of the rainy season. The need of change is born in the Arabian nature. The roving disposition which these nomads inherited from their ancestors makes of their city life a mere exchange from the tents in the desert; and if they cannot change their encampment, as in the olden times, they can at least fold up their tents figuratively, and build a new house. The last Master of Egypt, Ismail Pasha, was a great architect, possessing the fever of construction to such a degree that we owe to his building mania the bounteous luxuriance of thirty palaces with magnificent gardens, each having a separate shady beauty of its own; besides hundreds of barracks hardly distinguishable from the palaces, as well as schools, mosques, and hospitals, all as costly as they are ugly and vulgar. The expense and difficulty of transportation forced Ismail to depend on what his immediate vicinity produced in the way of material for constructing these new monuments to his glorious reign. At every turn the ancient mosques, as well as the public and private buildings, furnished for his palaces exquisitely chiselled stone-work, mushrebîyehs, windows carved like spider-webs in cedar, fountains of rose marble, colonnades of granite and balconies of sculptured work, making up in some degree for the shortcomings of the Parisian furniture of the most gaudy and detestable description, which was palmed off on the unsuspecting Khedive for several millions of francs, to decorate the interior of his royal harems.

The Rue de Rivoli is the Place de la Concorde of Cairo; that is to say, it is the spot most permeated with life and color. It has undergone many changes. Once a beautiful lake surrounded by shady walks, the wonder of the Oriental world, it is now a simple garden planted with tropical growth, and filled with rare plants and bright-plumaged birds, surrounding an open square and the European Theatre. As soon as four o'clock strikes, the gay world of Cairo promenades in the garden, enjoying the music of the Citadel military band and the coolness of the evening, and then goes forth in open victorias driven by dark-skinned and red-turbaned coachmen, who guide their high-spirited horses along the acacia-bordered avenue towards the Ghesireh Palace or the beautiful road to Shubra.

At nine o'clock in the evening, an Italian opera just across the park allures all tourist Cairo during the season, if the seductive charm of the "moonbeam's smile" that Browning talks about, and the delicious reflection of it on mosques and fairy balconies, with the scents from a hundred garden flowers, and the mysterious, ever-changing Eastern night scenes do not make the real drama and living scenery viewed from the open terrace more enchanting than the airs from "Aïda" or "Madame Angot."

The European quarter is a town built during our generation of pleasure-seekers and officials, "whose spirit is always visible in their masonry." Not displeasing, however, are the pretty attempts at Arabic architectural imitations of several new Oriental houses, some of them containing valuable curios and collections of Egyptian antiquities. An artistic Frenchman has built a veritable *chef d'œuvre* of an Arabian house, but the greater part of the buildings are Italian, with endless flat walls and sky-blue shutters, surrounded by gardens extending along well-kept boulevards, which are lighted with gas. Here and there an immense hotel blooms out in its pink stucco brilliancy from the tall surroundings of feathery palms and the heavy foliage of the Mimosa Nilotica trees. The Hotel Continental close by the official residence of Lord Cromer is a Mecca for our English cousins; the splendid ball-room is lined with large mirrors, where each one of them can look upon himself with pleasure; and two evenings in every week these mirrors reflect the British nobility in very tasteless ball-gowns, which do not shock us so much when we consider how many unenlightened notions, of more important bearing on modern customs, are always visible in the outward appearance of these worn-out institutions of caste. The modern knights-errant are not exactly mail-clad, as of old, but the heavy braided and gilded military dress and side arms aid the resemblance of these gatherings to the last-century pictures in the National Gallery.

Shubra is the modern palace of the Khedive, but has nothing distinctly artistic to recommend it; nor is it splendid enough to resemble a royal residence in any detail. A plain, prosaic structure, utterly devoid of design or pretension to architecture, it belongs to what some one has called "stone waste paper." It is the residence of the queen mother, — the Khedevine, as she is called, — and also of Abbas II.

The beautiful road to Shubra was long ago a lovely avenue shaded with leafy trees and bordered with orange gardens; perhaps nothing in the world was to be compared to it until the mighty sycamores, not yet forty years old, and which live in this climate three centuries, were shorn of their beautiful feathery branches for firewood. Now the tangled hedges, allowed to grow in rank luxuriance, intercept your way to the palm thickets, and hide from sight the orange and lemon groves; but the sugar-cane fields are still there, the sunset tints the tamarinds as far as the yellow desert, and long strings of camels undulate in single file over the boundless sand, merging in the distant perspective like an elongated kite's tail fallen out of the sky. The carriages of popular Pashas and rich Effendis crowd the Shubra Avenue on Mohammedan fête-days. A great deal of imagination is necessary to discover the beauty of these waxen inmates, whose dark eyes are accentuated with kohol; and the full moon face, which is the ideal of a Turkish Venus, is mercifully veiled in white gauze, which refines the picture, framed by an English brougham.

In the Cairo Directory, the date of the birth of the present Khedive is given as occurring 1 Gamad Akher, 1291, — rather a startling announcement to an eye accustomed to the Gregorian calendar. In the same Directory are given the names and dates of the "famille Khedéviale."

Son Altesse, Abbas II., Khédive d'Egypte, élévement au Trône 8 Gamad, 1309. January 8th, 1892.

S. A. la Princesse Emma Hanem, mère de son Altesse le Khédive.

S. A. le Prince Mehemet Ali frère de son Altesse le Khédive.

S. A. la Princesse Hadgi Nanem.

The grandson of Mehemet Ali, who founded modern Egypt, and created its institutions, laws, customs, and government, is as much a democrat to all outward appearances as a radical German. A slightly built young man just turned twenty-one years, he looks much too young to assume the duties and responsibilities of governing. This new-fashioned Pharaoh knows little and cares less for the imposing and elaborate machinery of court ceremonial and millinery. Every morning at ten o'clock he drives to the Abbidin Palace in a plain victoria drawn by two black horses; he is dressed like any English gentleman, with the single exception of an orthodox red turban, which he constantly lifts to acknowledge the greetings of the people; without pomp or ceremony he returns from business at five o'clock, having spent the day at his desk in the modest, but comfortable offices of the palace.

Abbas II. is an enigma to all Cairo; he has not received or entertained what is called society since he ascended the throne, but has well amused himself by instituting changes and upsetting the politics and established order of things, and has yet to learn the lesson that "le roi règne, mais il ne gouverne pas." The ministry have not even succeeded in their traditional right of choosing a bride; and the young man having taken unto himself a political family, he may end in following out the same privilege in his heart affairs, and select his own wife.

Friday at twelve a modest escort of four native cavalrymen precede the Khedive's carriage *en route* to his favorite mosque, or perhaps to the citadel of Mehemet Ali, where Lord Cromer's "Black Watch" lean far out over the barrack balconies idling away the uneventful hours in the same fancied security as the Mamelukes who were exterminated on this very spot by a Turkish despot with a cruel and cunning revenge, which suddenly made a barbarian of the ancestor of this young sovereign, who is not more seemingly in love with British occupation than was his predecessor with his Circassian Mamelukes.

GIZEH.

THE weather in Cairo is always fine during the season, which eliminates one very popular topic of conversation among the winter guests. Rain and fog are never considered as hindrances to any proposed *fête champêtre,* for the sun shines on perpetually with singular softness, the rays apparently passing through a screen of delicate tissues, which tempers its heat and absorbs its light. No one has a moment to waste; and the slowness of the *table d'hôte* breakfast is a great annoyance, especially as the Cairene conception of a *cuisine* leaves much to be desired. We are never less than an hour and a half at this occupation, which, however, does not interfere with the discussion of various plans for the afternoon. What are you going to see to-day? is the question passed from one to another down the long dining-room, and the interminable intervals between the courses are bridged over by an *entente cordiale* prevailing among the representatives of all countries on this absorbing subject of sight-seeing. The new-comers have invariably planned out a day according to

Baedeker, consisting in a summing up of seventy Cairene sights, and dividing them by six hard working days of eight hours each,— including mosques, pyramids, bazaars, and Heliopolis, the tombs of the Khedives, and the Virgin's Tree, in bewildering confusion.

The usual way to do the Museum is to take it, in tourist's terms, on the way to the pyramids; and a shudder went through me at this irreverent manner of rushing past the dead Pharaohs, the repose of their restful sleep contrasting serenely with the pushing crowd of scurrying tourists. We scorned the accepted method, and reserved our admiration exclusively for the venerable dust of Egyptian dynasties at Gizeh. Outside, on the pavement, a horde of Turks had long lain "dreaming of the hour" which would bring piastres for donkey hire. Aroused by our appearance at the hotel entrance, the blue burnooses and turbaned heads immediately blended into fantastic groups of Arabic design,— an animated pyramid of bright-faced and delicate-featured bronzes, each offering his patient beast for the excursion, or clamoring to be employed as driver of a team of discouraged-looking horses on the opposite side of the street, for which the usual price was demanded, plus an amount of piastres added or diminished from the official carriage rates printed inside the vehicle, according to the idea formed of your liberality or indifference. The porter always appears as a deliverer at this moment, and declares the carriage fare for Lel Antikat (the Museum of Antiquities) to be twelve piastres to go and return, eight piastres an hour while you wait. "Tarrifa," murmurs the dispersing crowd, who have nothing more to say, and a carriage awaits your pleasure.

The Museum of Gizeh is reached by the new iron bridge over the Nile. The road is well kept, and is shaded by beautiful lebbek-trees, and the tall grasses of the sugar-cane are all shooting and waving in the breeze, which lightly stirs the heavy clover, bends the yellow mustard flowers, and then ripples the gray water along the river-side, where the white herons are snapping their prey, half-hidden by the bulrushes.

We had started in company with an involuntary escort of donkeys ridden by barefoot Arabs, which soon disappeared amid the temptations of the sugar-cane bazaar. Occasionally a Turkish soldier going to the races passed, dressed in an embroidered red and gold costume marvellously combined with silks and silver, producing a harmonious effect at once beautiful and splendidly savage. A saïs in loose fluttering white trousers, a bright gold jacket with puffed crêpe sleeves, a tight turban with black silk tassel streaming to the waist, scarcely touching his bare feet to the earth, he throws back his shoulders, and with a slender pole erect in his hand, clears the way for his master's high-stepping horse and English dog-cart, impeded by a string of the discarded camels, once the thoroughbreds of Egypt, but who now carry the fellâhîn with the same grace as they did the Pharaohs.

After a short half-hour, I learned we were passing Roda, the island of the episode of Moses in the bulrushes; and soon, through a garden of tall shrubs and grand old trees, is seen the third and last "eternal dwelling-place" of the Pharaohs. In their vain imaginings, the artists of the Rameseum at Thebes, upon whose portals were carved the adder guardians of the door of heaven, inscribed a legend that these pictured tombs should be the last and final resting-place of the kings. There seems a probability now that in the course of time their mortal remains will be set down as many times as Queen Eleanor's coffin, in face of the fact that they have suffered re-entombment twice in five years,—first at Boulak, and then at Gizeh, and in a stucco building, a material they would have scoffed at during their age of stone.

A few years ago, the Museum of Egyptian Antiquities at Boulak was transferred to the vice-regal palace at Gizeh on the banks of the Nile, and this modern building gleams out of a luxurious garden, — a fit setting for the treasures and relics of the kings and princes, whose imperial ideas of beauty are far surpassed by the magnificence of the tree ferns and flowers of the rarely ornamented garden grounds.

There is little to relate that is not contained in the hand-book sold at the entrance for two piastres. I soon lost myself in the restfulness and silence of the quiet halls, where the dumb and stony inmates speak a sign language understood by savants, but only comprehended in a sort of intuitive way by a woman's fancy.

The first of the great apartments on the entrance floor of the museum is the "Salle de l'Ancien Empire," which is said to contain the largest existing collection of monuments of the primeval empire. We are in the presence of the builders of the pyramids of Medum. A notice, pasted at the foot of a glass case, declares the occupant sitting there in stony indifference, one hand resting on each smooth and rounded knee, to be Prince Rahotep, and the delicate-featured woman by his side is the royal princess Nefert "the beautiful," the wife of Rahotep, son of Senferu, "the commander of the king's warriors, chief of the temple city of Heliopolis, the town of the god Ra." Of fair and faintly tinted skin, clad in fine white linen garments, and wearing a slender circlet of ribbon about her head;

her short frizzled hair arranged in a wig (a fairly good one for ancient Egypt); the delicate white feet bare, with imperceptible ankles. Before you is a perfect picture of an ancient Egyptian beauty. The marvellous liquid eyes, made of quartz upon a background of silver, haunt you, and are the amazement of all who look upon the oldest statue in the world.

The pyramids of Gizeh had not been built when these statues were hewn out of stone to adorn the tomb-chambers near the Medum Pyramids on the Nile.

It was the tender, careful hands of Mariette Bey, the great French savant, who first excavated the necropolis tomb-chambers, mastabas, and pyramids of King Senferu, which contained the most interesting monuments in existence of the handicraft of the third and fourth dynasty. Senferu, the founder of the fourth dynasty, and the first king of whom we possess any contemporaneous monuments, was the builder of the shining pyramid which he called the "Pyramid of the Rising," whose terraces of yellow stone form a gleaming mountain of masonry on the border of the brown desert fifty miles south of Cairo. Of this old-world king it was written in ancient papyrus, "Then was raised up the holiness of King Senferu as a good king over the whole country," and he, rejoicing during his life in the title of "The Maker of Good" and "the Lord of Truth," was determined to eclipse "the tombs of all who went before or after, and keep his body safe, his name secure through all ages."

A modern traveller describes a visit to Flinders Petrie, who finished the work of excavation begun by Mariette Bey; the account is full of interesting details of the dangers and difficulties of uncovering the mastabas pits of the family of Senferu at the Medum Pyramid. He relates that if one wished to see Flinders Petrie at work under the shadow of the pyramid, he would be found in a tiny tent, an old packing-box serving alike as table and chair; a box of biscuits, some potted-meat cans, and a paraffine stove making up the dining and drawing room furniture of the brave explorer's rough reed hut, close to the old monuments which are yielding up their secrets to him; and should you enter the little tomb adjoining, where once, with much lamentation and many cakes of offering, those entered who mourned for Nefer Mat, you will see a rude camp bedstead. There, at the end of long days of digging, sleeps the explorer, and "the stars can look in upon him and the first sun visit him."

During the excavation, the most friendly relations existed between the fellah laborers and the "Khanaja Engleese," the English gentleman. They all loved him; and the master and the men seemed bound by a tie too uncommon among the Thebes and Karnak authorities, who use the kourbash so severely on the naked ankles of men, women, and children, lashing them with elephant-hide whips when the poor creatures falter under the weight of their heavy palm baskets of mould, and half faint under the strain of hard work for ten hours a day with the summer sun at over a hundred degrees.

Among the remarkable discoveries of Mr. Petrie, not the least interesting were the mastaba graves, showing two apparently different modes of burial at the same age and side by side. In his interesting book, "Ten Years Digging in Egypt," Mr. Petrie writes, —

"Another glimpse of the prehistoric age of Egypt is afforded by the burials at Medum. The later people always buried at full length, and with some provision for the body, such as food, head-rests, etc. Such burials are found among the nobles at Medum; but most of the people there were buried in a contracted form, nose and knees, or at least with the thigh bent square with the body and heels drawn up. And, moreover, no food, vessels, or other objects are put in. Yet there was no more difference shown; the bodies are in deep well tombs, often placed in large wooden boxes, which must have been valuable in Egypt, and always lying with the head to the north, facing the East. Here is clearly a total difference in beliefs, and probably in race. We know that two races, the aquiline-nosed and the snouty, can be distinguished in early times; and it seems that the aborigines used the contracted burial, and the dynastic race the extended burial, which, with its customs, soon became the national mode.

"Is it likely that the bulk of the people should have resisted this change for some eight hundred years, and then have suddenly adopted it in two or three generations? Does not this rapid adoption of the upper-class custom, between the beginning of the fourth dynasty and the immediately succeeding times suggest that the dynastic race did not enter Egypt until shortly before we find their monuments? At least, the notion that the stages preceding the known monuments should be sought outside of Egypt, and that this is the explanation of the dearth of objects before the fourth dynasty, is strengthened by the change of custom and belief we then find."

The descendants of King Senferu, the Lady Atot and Nefer Mat, and also Rahotep, and the Princess Nefert of Gizeh fame, were possessed with a mania for mastabas; and the wonderful beauty of the cutting and enamelling of their stone sculptures lends a strange interest to the tombs, and from these sanctuary pictures it comes to pass that every minutiæ of their lives is known to us as perfectly as if five thousand suns had not tried in vain to throw an eternal shade on them. The drawings show us Nefer Mat was a great farmer, besides, and that each of the tenants of his vast estate had sent a servant with offerings to his tomb; that he was also a mighty hunter, for the hunting hawks sculptured above the door of the tomb-chamber have "perched and sat, and nothing more," for thirty-five hundred centuries.

The Lady Atot was also a lover of sport, perhaps sharpened by the "idlesse" of an Egyptian lady's monotonous existence, for the Gizeh Museum stone pictures show how she diversified her lotus-eating days. On a façade taken from her tomb, men are represented as engaged in snaring wild fowl with a large net, while three Egyptians bring the game they have captured to the princess with great ceremony, and the inscription relates that "the Lady Atot receives with pleasure the game caught alive by the chief noble, Nefer Mat."

Hardly less interesting as illustrating the domestic side of this Egyptian lady's accomplishments is the exquisite fresco of geese in the same treasure-room of Gizeh Museum; the six fowls are drawn and colored with the greatest skill and accuracy, each feather finished as carefully as a perfect miniature painting on a material of hardened clay coated with plaster of Paris. And so in the early dawn of history we find that a love of field sports was not inconsistent with a taste for homely farm-yard duties, in spite of all legends to the contrary. In fact, with princes as farmers and noble ladies tending fowls, the old couplet comes to mind, —

"When Adam delved and Eve span,
Who was then the gentleman?"

But it is the happy family life of Nefer Mat's time which charms us most; we see the brave Egyptian going forth to war in his gilded and enamelled chariot; a picture follows where he is portrayed slaying his foes, and then, returning home laden with trophies, to be welcomed and greeted by his affectionate family. At dinner they are all enjoying the good things prepared for them, the sons and daughters entertaining the guests, while musicians are playing on various instruments, harps, lutes, guitars, cymbals, and flutes in the most methodical, common-place manner. In this admirable domesticity of the fourth dynasty, and the thirtieth degree of latitude, a father called his daughter "sweetheart," and the girl phrases her reply in affectionate language to the "Best Beloved."

And this was in the reign of Rahotep, the king, in the very beginning of things.

The "Salle de l'Ancien Empire" is followed by an endless stretch of stone chambers, whose walls are lined with cabinets containing an army of figures of Egyptian priests, royal scribes, sacred serpents and sceptres in limestone, bronze, and gray granite. An inscription describes a small figure "as the steward of the grain for tribute, Nefer;" but for other reasons than respect for his stewardship is the granite valued and preserved by the antiquarian of the nineteenth century. It happens that the artist who immortalized Nefer is himself forgotten, but his work remains as one of the finest existing specimens of Egyptian sculpture. It is indeed a wonderful thing to be carried back to the first ages of the world, but still more puzzling to find a race who, having reached a most enviable position in all the arts, have even mastered the mysteries of the sciences which we, the heirs of all the ages, are still vainly struggling with.

In the "Salle Funéraire" are the cases of scarabs found in the bodies of mummies where the heart has been removed. Scarabs in glass, and in cornelian and perforated wood and enamel, some jewelled and some true beetles, are now seen in the open daylight after their long and grewsome entombment. The enlightened sentiments and subtle foresight of these old philosophers speak out to us from these symbols of a future life, which prove, without a doubt, that they believed in a resurrection from the dead. C. F. Gordon-Cummings says that, —

"The lesson was learned from the little beetle mother who lays her eggs on the damp earth of the Nile banks, and then, depositing layers of clay above them and cutting away the earth beneath, till she has fashioned a round clay ball in the heart of which her eggs are safely imbedded, slowly and patiently moves backwards, rolling this precious ball to the edge of the desert, where, in the warm, dry sand, she excavates a long gallery, wherein, as in a catacomb, she buries herself, carrying with her the clay ball, wherein so many germs of life lie hidden and protected. Thence, in due time, a multitude of tiny living creatures come forth to crawl through their little span of existence, thereafter to fall asleep in mummy-like chrysalis, and await the wondrous day when they shall come forth from thence, in a new and perfect form, no longer hideous worms, grubbing underground or crawling miserably in the desert, but beautiful beetles, clad in armor of emerald and gold, and endowed with delicate wings and power of swift movement on earth or in air.

"What marvel that these old philosophers beheld, in all this subtle foresight, a trace of divine wisdom? — that they should adopt the beetle, with its earth globe filled with the seed of life, as the most meet symbol of the Creator of this round world, with all its wondrous forms of beings? When, too, in that carefully excavated tomb, with its long gallery, and in the swathed chrysalis whence the sleeper arose in a wholly new form and endowed with new powers, they found Nature's own example for constructing great catacombs wherein they hid their precious mummied dead, to await their reappearance on this earth in some wholly new condition, — an emblem, they believed, not merely of resurrection, but also of transmigration."

In some of the hieroglyphics, the scarab is seen helping the soul heavenward. Thus, when a funeral boat finds its passage to the holy lake barred by a bridge, this kindly beetle is shown, hanging from heaven by its hind legs, while with its fore claws it raises the bridge, and so allows the boat to pass. This scene typifies the resurrection.

The manufacture of scarabs and funeral beads is carried on with great industry at Birmington, and in spite of repeated experiences of the fictitious character of various mouldy and ancient-looking beetles sold on the street of Cairo, the temptation to buy is occasionally too strong for prudence. On rare occasions it happens that a tourist who has been weak enough to yield to an offer of a royal cartouche for five piastres, finds that he has bought a real antique, worth at least twenty-five pounds in London.

The profit in mummies has also promoted their manufacture in myriads at Luxor, whence they are sent to all countries. We are told that one firm alone manufactures hundreds for a prominent museum, and tickets them Rameses or Pharaoh, "according to demand."

One made of an animal skin, and wrapped in the conventional yellow linen bands, was only six months old when it went to an American circus, which undoubtedly heralded its arrival in flaming posters as "guaranteed genuine."

But this is only the first stage in the catalogue of antiquities. Farther on are the quaintest little treasures of the museum,— the ornaments of an Egyptian lady's dressing-tables, little boxes for the kohol, which ladies used some centuries ago to enhance the beauty of their eyes, — just as modern beauties of Cairo do to-day; or a dainty covered wooden case for perfume, the handle a female figure in the act of swimming, holding in her outstretched hands a duck, the body of which is hollowed to receive the perfumery, while the wings form the cover; and prettiest of all, a gilded fan, delicately fashioned, with the holes still visible which held the ostrich feathers with which it was originally furnished. On the mural paintings, every detail of fashion is depicted with the accuracy of a modern "Ladies' Book," the trimmings, the furbelows, and head-gear then in vogue, even to the latest Theban patterns in couches and Luxor chairs. We know also that a wig was considered the proper thing for the grand dames of the fourth dynasty, as you may see one for yourself on the shelves of the Gizeh Museum. There is nothing which palls on me so soon as a great numbered case of ancient jewelry, and I seem to see them yet in their yellowed invaluableness,— these crushed and beaten bracelets and amulets labelled the "Jewels of Queen Hahhotep." It is very wrong, I know, to pass over them with so little notice, but my lack of enthusiasm and devotion was supplied by half-a-dozen of the fair sex, who will speak very affectionately of the glittering diadems and superb bracelets next winter, as they cluster around a log fire in some far-distant New England home.

Through the great rooms built in a serious style, and whose beauty consists in massive solidity, filled with statuettes and images of sacred animals, — "bleating gods," as they are called by an English poet, — we finally reach the celebrated sculptures of the Hyksos period, finding that each of these great kings has an expression peculiarly his own, the personality asserting itself in the individuality of his postures, the gifts he presents to his tutelary goddess, and the traces of pride and conquest the stern physiognomy represents. Nowhere does an Ethiopian face obtrude itself; and the portrait heads of the sphinx kings are of the Semitic, Arabian, or Shepherd types, representing the races who finally became so powerful that they overthrew the armies of the Pharaohs and became masters of the whole of lower Egypt. So it happened that when Joseph came to Egypt he found on the throne a monarch of a race kindred to his own, although maintaining the customs and ancient laws of the Pharaohs. At El Kat there is an inscription very legible on an ancient sepulchre which makes mention of a famine, perhaps identical with the one which brought the patriarch Jacob and his family to Egypt. This tomb was built by a naval officer, father of Aahmes I., who embellished Thebes, the

Hyksos capital, with magnificent edifices, about four centuries before the exodus.

The engraved inscription runs like this: "When a famine prevailed for many years, then I gave them the city corn during each famine."

Very little has been said concerning the coal-black granite bust with a wing-shaped wig, undoubtedly that of the "new king" which "knew not Joseph;" it is certainly a strange sensation to behold his face carved in granite, worthy of high-wrought sentiment and serious contemplation, but it may well startle you to be told that in a few moments you will be in his actual presence.

When one is brought face to face with the very bodies of the mightiest of earth's princes, of whose cruel oppression one has heard from childhood, a traditional awe seizes you; and you fear lest the dead should only be dissembling, and, resenting perhaps your curious gazing, step down from their glass cases and suddenly appear in their old seats of power. Mentally reviving the past and seriously retrospecting, is apt to result in reaction to the comical side of our composite nature; and I found myself roused from a dreamy revery and once more in the Christian present, for a crowd of Cook's tourists, who evidently had neglected their early Biblical education, were rushing hastily about, glancing at the printed inscriptions on the withered royal mummies in a search of the Pharaoh who is supposed by all good people to be at the bottom of the Red Sea. However, the inherent seriousness of the open coffins of the ancient kings had the effect of checking to a certain degree the usual tourist mockery.

It is written of the mighty sepulchres at Thebes and Memphis that "the kings of the nation lie in glory, every one in his own house;" for if there was one thing dearer than another to a Pharaoh, it was these glorious tombs, and nothing could have been more bitter to these exclusive aristocrats than the idea of a communistic graveyard in a civilized palace, for the mummy-cases of priests and potentates are all ticketed alike and numbered, to aid the curious tourist to accomplish the very evil they most dreaded, the insulting scrutiny of the bodies of their dead.

The process of mummification, or embalming of the bodies, of wealthy Egyptians was a very costly affair; it is described as occupying three months, during which the different organs — the heart, liver, etc. — were removed, packed in separate vases, and committed to the especial care of the Four Guardians of Hades. The cavity was then filled with gums and costly spices from Araby, and strips of linen dipped in myrrh were wrapped about the body, every limb and joint being swathed completely and with great skill, as some of these strips are found to be actually a thousand yards long. Having then gilded and decorated the thick layers of cloth, the pasteboard was laid on, when it was dampened to take the impress of the human figure. The artists skilfully painted it with hieroglyphics, which told the story of the lifeless body within, and a stone sarcophagus received the mummy, and a programme of the final ceremonies of the day of judgment.

In some cases, the body, swathed in linen, lies exposed in the mummy-case, which is modelled to represent the head and figure of the dead one. The feet are generally bare, and, as in Pharaoh's case, are revealed to each curious gazer, while Ebers speaks of a mummy the soles of whose feet had been removed, in order to spare the dread halls of Amenti from being soiled in passing through them. Amulets and precious stones were also deposited among the bandages, — an especially valuable one doing duty for the heart.

Of all the hundreds of ancient temples that spring up in stony magnificence on the narrow green belt of soil which we call Egypt, each one, no matter how provincial in other respects, had its establishment for the process of mummification.[1] A dead Egyptian, after being given over to priestly

---

[1] For the details of Egyptian burial I am indebted to C. F. Gordon-Cummings.

embalmers, was restored at the end of seventy days to his disconsolate family, who disposed of him in a cupboard until such time as the finances of the friends warranted an expensive funeral, when the "family skeleton" was brought out of the hidden place, and the relatives having assembled, a procession was formed, when the offerings of ointment, wines, and golden images, which accompanied the mummy to the "Sacred Lake," were carried as usual by women throwing dust on their heads and beating their breasts courageously, strengthened, we are told, by no other draught than that from the amphora of their affection.

The soul's passage through the regions of the dead is described and pictured in the Liturgy of the Dead, which was the great literary glory of the old Egyptian religion.

In one of the chapters of this remarkable book, an Osirian *lit de justice* is introduced, managed by forty-two Assessors, holding court by the side of a sacred lake, artificially made for this purpose in every Egyptian province. A venerable predecessor of the Greek Charon was appointed to ferry over the dead soul *en route* to his place in the family vault. Before this coveted desideratum could be accomplished, the solemn ordeal of trial before Osiris was to be undergone. The questions of this minister for spiritual affairs were directed towards the omission and commission of such sins as would be equally grievous in the nineteenth century, the crimes to be answered were rigidly inquired into by each of the forty-two avenging accusers, and the plaintiff spirit thus states his case to one: "O thou who dost crack the bones, I have not lied;" "O thou with flaming eyes, I have not played the hypocrite." To another he answers, "I have not been a drunkard." "I have not blasphemed the gods, nor been undutiful, nor sworn falsely." This is the soul's side of the case, spoken in self-defence. While listening to the oratory, the judges take the precaution of securing direct evidence, and order the heart to be weighed in the balance, held by Horus the Dawn, son of Osiris.

If proven guilty, the defendant's mummy was not permitted to enter on the last voyage in the sacred boat, but was doomed to leave Paradise, and, not even allowed to stand disconsolately at the gate, like the Peri, was compelled to transmigrate into the form of that animal which his character most resembled while on earth, if not condemned to suffer the more shameful fate of a return to the position of skeleton in a closet, while the disgraced family found the means of atoning financially for his misdoings. Should the deceased have been falsely accused, grave penalties are attached to his heavenly prosecutor; and the happy mummy enters the "Ship of God" and sails along the Ocean of Infinity, taking the shape most agreeable to himself, his final entrance to the tomb-chamber on the opposite bank of the lake being typical of the redeemed one's gaining his rest in a celestial home, "where the lotus and the flowery reeds are forever in blossom." "Here they reap the corn and reap the fruits under the eyes and smile of the Lord of Joy, who exhorts them thus: 'Take your sickles, reap your grain, carry it into your dwellings, that ye may be glad therewith, and present it as a pure offering unto God.'" By inscriptions on ancient tombs we are told that the bodies of the occupants who found favor with the Great Judge, and have been acquitted, inhabit the tomb in blissful repose, while the "Anchiu" — that is, living ones — rejoice in the presence of their Creator. To an Egyptian, his palace was merely an inn, and the tomb his eternal dwelling-place, which did not, however, prevent the latter from being bought, sold, or exchanged as occasion and circumstances demanded; and owing to the fact that the eternal resting-places were in the hands of the priesthood, a great revenue was obtained from the forced sale of a family tomb to a more prosperous patron, who could better afford it.

That the justified ones enjoyed perpetual peace, and were considered the most fortunate possessors of the tree of life, the fruit of which made gods of all who tasted it, that they were destined to a glorious immortality, and not to be hopelessly mourned and regretted is evident from the cheerful funeral songs, actually chanted to harp accompaniment at the feasts of an ancient Egyptian.

The original of the following "Song of the Harper," according to H. D. Rawnsley, who quotes it, was found in the tomb of Neferhotep at Abbel-Kurnah, near Thebes, and is declared to be a good specimen of the poetry of the eighteenth dynasty. Neferhotep is represented sitting with his wife and sister, Renmi-m-ast-nek, his son Ptahmes and his daughter Ta-Khat standing by their side with the harper established in a seat, — doubtless one of those luxurious bronze chairs labelled 2364 in the Museum, feet and arms in the form of lions, and the back consisting of a hawk with outspread wings. The rhythmic words are addressed to the departed as well as the guests at his banquet, the poem assuming all the while that the former is still alive.

THE SONG OF THE HARPER.

1700–1400 B. C.

THIS is the song the harper used to sing
    In the tomb chapel of the Osirian,
The blessed Neferhotep, Amen's priest.

I.

Neferhotep, great and blest,
    Of a truth is sleeping;
We as surety for his rest,
    All good charges keeping.
Since the day when Ra and Tum
    Ran his first of races,
Fathers pass, and after come
    Children in their places.
Certain as great Ra appears,
    Sires are sons begetting,
Man begets, and woman bears,
    Sure as Tum is setting.
Breezes from the morning blown
    Every man inhaleth,
To his place then going down,
    Woman-born, he faileth.

II.

May this day in joy return,
    Speed it, holy father;
Scent these oils we pour and burn,
    Take the flowers we gather.
In thy heart, as in thy shrine,
    See thy sister dwelling;
Round her arms and bosom twine
    Lotus flowers, excelling.
Lo! she sits beside thee close;
    Let the harp delight thee;
Let our singing banish woes,
    Leave the cares that spite thee.

Joy thee till the pilgrim band
   One day shall have started,
Enter to thy silent land,
   Welcome, and long parted.

III.

That this day with joy may speed,
   Patriarch, grant assistance;
Whole of heart and pure of deed
   Past from Earth's existence.
His life shared the common lot,
   Here is no sure dwelling;
He who just now was, is not,
   And his place past telling.
So it has been since the sun
   Rose, so must be, O man!
Eyes just open, then as one
   Never born of woman.
In the shades, upon the brink
   Of the sacred river,
'Mid the ghosts thy soul doth drink
   Draughts of life forever.

IV.

If when harvest fails, the poor
   Cry to thee for feeding,
Give, so honored evermore
   Shall thy name be speeding.

Give, so to thy funeral feast
  Crowds will come, adoring;
In his panther skin, the priest
  Wine to thee outpouring.
Cakes of bread and staves of song
  Will be thine, elected
Stand before god Ra, the throng
  Of thy friends, protected.
Harvests duly shall return,
  Nor thy Shu forsaken;
While in hell the lost ones burn,
  Glorious shalt thou waken.

v.

Neferhotep, pure of hand,
  Speed the day, we pray thee;
Not the buildings thou hast planned
  Could avail to stay thee.
All his wealth this little earth
  For his rest containeth,
This poor ash is all his worth —
  Look ye! what remaineth.
When the moments came that he
  Sought the realms of heaven,
Not one jot might added be,
  Not one moment given.
They whose barns are crammed with corn,
  One day make a finish;
Death will laugh their wealth to scorn,
  Death their pride will 'minish.

VI.

Friends, ye all one day go hence;
    Be your hearts discerning;
Mind ye of the bourne from whence
    There is no returning.
Honest lives will then have proved
    Gain, but loathe transgressing;
Be ye just, for justice, loved,
    Brings a good man blessing.
Be we coward, be we brave,
    Rich in friends, forsaken:
None of us escape the grave, —
    All alike are taken.
Give of thine abundance, give,
    And to truth attending,
Blest by Isis shalt thou live
    Happy, to thine ending.

And so we come back to the vast, almost vacant salon, to the pink and gray mummies of a royal race, not one of whom lived after the year 1000 B. C. Ranged in a large circle, the gilded and painted cases gleaming like a sun-suffused corona under the bright central dome, Thothmes II., king of the eighteenth dynasty, Rameses III., founder of the twelfth dynasty, and then the mightiness of Rameses II., Pharaoh in the flesh, are before us in their Assyrian coffins, shaped as nearly as possible to fit the body, and elaborately decorated with golden hawks and winged emblems of royalty.

The original coffin of Rameses II. was destroyed about the twenty-first dynasty, according to an hieratic inscription, which relates that tomb inspectors visited the Rameseum as late as the year 1100. Some writings on papyrus lately discovered contain the information that the royal tombs were desecrated about that time, the gold was stolen, the sacred mummies, amulets, and ornaments taken without hesitation, while the modern sacrilege of body-snatching did not at all enter the plan of the robbers. After that, Pharaoh and his father, Seti I., were carried off and removed for safety to the tomb of Queen Ansera, which was also broken into, and the wandering mummies were bumped and rattled up the steep incline to the Valley of the Kings in the Theban mountains. It must be acknowledged that in stature, at least, Pharaoh was great indeed; his form nearly outlines the mummy-case where he lies, bound around with the yellow linen bands, a withered warrior, who in life measured six feet, three inches, in height. There is, however, about the blackened mould of the mighty king a good foundation to reconstruct his peculiarities of face and figure as they appeared in life. Half a glance would reveal the strength and character which lies in the high forehead, the dignity of chin and mouth, and the strange and sinister expression of the beaked nose of the Hebraic type, singularly like unto the aged, hoary expression of the unfeathered beak of a young crow. However, beyond the fact of his gray hairs, and eyebrows like dandelion down, the straight back and powerful shoulders give little hint of an old man who has passed the limit of his threescore years and ten. And this is the charred *débris* of the wonderful man who lights up the poetry of Pen-ta-tur into images of radiant splendor; addressed by the bard as "gracious Lord" and "bravest King," "Savior," "Guard of Egypt in the battle," the Pharaoh who, in the conflict with the Khita, uprose like a sun-god, donned his armor and mighty weapons, and with the noble horses, "Victory of Thebes," dashed alone into the midst of the fray, calling on his Father Ammon to remember the noble monuments and temples dedicated to him which should stand a thousand years, the "tall gates and wondrous works beside the Nile to last until eternity, the obelisks conveyed from Elephantin's Isle, to remember also who sent ships upon the sea, to pour wealth into the temple's treasury, and to remember him who commanded these things, and who now beseeches the Lord's favor and help in his time of necessity, knowing that Ammon's grace is better far to me than a million fighting men and ten thousand chariots be."

And Ammon, lover of a brave heart, finding a spirit he could rejoice in, hastened to the mighty child of earth and fought with him, standing beside him, hurling the darts and saving the blades until the horsemen of Khita land sank in the water of Arunsha's tide, as crocodiles fall from a bank, while the chief's enemies and their king were left alone. None escaped who put not their trust in Ammon, for the poem[1] ends with the words of Pharaoh: "I slew, I slew, and slew."

But Rameses II., beloved of Ra, the sun-god, is most interesting in another and more familiar rôle as the Pharaoh of the oppression, — the "new king over Egypt which knew not Joseph." Brugsch Bey, in 1881, brought to Cairo the sheeted corpse of the man who issued an order to the taskmasters, the armed police of Egypt, relating to the Israelites, which for relentless cruelty holds its own without fear or favor against any *lettre de cachet* in modern times.

It was these bituminous lips that framed the decree for the murder of the innocents, not less selfishly than Herod the Great, who feared his kingdom menaced by another child of Israel, and it was this presence from whom the Hebrews appealed to their God, "who heard their sorrowings, and remembered his covenant with Abraham, with Isaac, and with Jacob." His feet have been

---

[1] Heroic Poem of Pen-ta-ur, 1326 B. C., relating the victory of Rameses II. over the Khita, 1328 B. C.

rubbed with henna, the red dye which blooms on the finger-tips of modern Egyptians, and they display, besides, great strength at the ankles. The guide with accustomed eyes noticed for us the wound in the side made by the priest who replaced the human heart of Pharaoh with one equally as stony and made of cornelian. So this is Pharaoh in his death-chamber; once the little boy child of the wall picture of Karnak, fighting by the side of his father Seti, who now lies so peacefully beside him, the warrior energies so plainly carved in the stern features and lurking still in the desiccated frame of the best-preserved mummy at Gizeh.

ON THE NILE.

FROM A CAIRO JOURNAL.

WHAT are the Cairene bazaars like? Well, nothing that I had imagined. Until I saw them, I was under the impression that the Turks were a silent and impassive race,— travellers usually say so; but the rush, the excitement, the shouting, and the resistless sweep of humanity in a narrow bazaar would humble a French boulevard. Stooping under the flapping awnings in the street of the spice merchants this morning, I followed the dragoman into the dusky-tinted atmosphere of the long lane of perfume booths, where the sweet scents of Araby and the precious attar of rose in large and small jars are stored away on the shelves which line the little draped dukkan, usually a recess only about six feet in width, freighted with smoke and the oppressive smell of dried flowers. We sit down on a bare wooden platform nearly waist high, without rug or mat, and the very counterfeit of its neighbors for a good distance on either side.

The shop is open to the street, and a curtain now looped aside answers for a door when the owner

goes to his dinner or his devotions. Glass jars of the apothecary type, containing ambergris, sandal-wood, and attar-of-rose essences, usually share the opposite shelves, and nowhere in the world does shopping become so fascinating an amusement as in these scented regions. The Arab has never learned that time is money; and his patience and delightful coffee, combined with honeyed phrases, make the long séance, which every purchase entails, a real pleasure. Before the compliments and coffee have ceased, you begin with the greatest assumed indifference the bargaining for the bright-colored bottles with their thousand rose leaves compressed into so many golden drops; then having been informed of the price of what pleases you most, a little word easily learned, and repeated in an ascending scale, denotes your astonishment at the sum demanded: la! la! la! you cry, each time more negatively than before. It sometimes takes two or three days for the most trifling purchase, and innumerable visits and white ribbon stirrup-cups besides, until the neighboring merchants begin to know you, and salaam with friendly interest, but, loyally enough, do not offer to tempt you away from your own particular dealer, who sits contentedly on the mastaba seat, smoking his nargileh in confidence. "Saib, Saib" (Very well, I'll take it); "Min Shanah" (For thy sake), he says at last, accepting several piastres less than his "denier prix" of the day before; then if it is the precious attar of rose which is in question, the test is applied, and to assure oneself the article is genuine, a drop is burned on a piece of tissue paper. If real, not a trace of the liquid is left to stain the paper. Inscriptions over many Arabian shops fail to indicate the business transacted over the coffee cups; it is customary to inscribe Korân phrases, which shine so calmly over the petty cacklings of the commercial world below them. "O Allah! thou who helpest us in want!" "O Allah! thou who openest the gates of profit!" These exclamations are often heard on opening the shops in the morning, and are repeated frequently with a view to facilitate the sales. I have heard that shopkeepers also use the most endearing terms on the most uncalled for occasions; fortunately these phrases are reserved for the natives, or one does not understand them. On a ledge of wood protruding into the street of the silver bazaar, crouches a fellah-woman shrouded in an indigo sheet, her elbows touching her knees, holding her black-veiled face in her two copper-colored hands, weighted with golden rings. Solitary as an "eagle on his chosen peak," she is viewing the heavy anklets and bracelets which will be her little daughter's wedding portion, while the booth is lighted up with glittering bawbles. From his corner in the depths of the den, the Arab is tempting his veiled customer. "Oh, my eyes, look here!" and "You sweet dear one!" he cooes, protesting disinterested interest, with tender words. What the effect of this is on the intended purchaser, one cannot judge. The eyes alone are uncovered, and they tell nothing; a long black yashmak covers the other features entirely. The woman's thoughts flutter among the ornaments, then with surprising swiftness she swoops down from her perch, picks over and selects her jewelry, which is tied in pink paper and borne away to a mud village in the depths of a cavernous pocket, which, unsuspected, is concealed under her linen drapery.

The bazaars of Cairo are long corridors, where carriages may not venture; but if you go on a donkey, or if walking, you are almost able to touch the opposite walls with extended arms. Each bazaar is a quarter devoted to its particular trade. The money-changers have theirs; the leather merchants also; and the carpet-dealers wax fat and sleek in their separate *sharia*, set on each side with the familiar raspberry and blue rugs, woven in the mellow combinations of green, red, and yellow, which Nature taught the East in the beginning of the world. The old commercial centre of Cairo, Khân el-Khalîlî, is a labyrinth possessing neither beginning nor end. You come across streets banked with Persian pottery and beautiful jewels, emerging into lanes filled with barbarous concoctions of pumpkin and cucumbers, which act like a violent discord as they greet the olfactory nerve; still those narrow tracks where the houses join in perspective overhead, from their great height, give shade, and bright awnings protect alike the proprietor of a *café* or a tinker in brass, and are all they require. The narrow streets are wide enough for a foot passenger, for the Arabs rarely use a carriage; and the shops of six or seven feet in width are quite large enough for the accommodation of the two or more purchasers in their sleepy transactions. When the old order changes in Cairo, it is to be hoped the new will not creep into the shops, so Oriental, picturesque, and beautifully adapted to their use, end, and aim.

The mosques of Cairo make splendid pictures. The camera will not betray crumbling pinnacles, ruined fountains, or the gray *débris* of fallen columns. A photograph of the mosque of Tooloon shows the beautiful arcades separated by pillars covered with the most exquisite ornamentation, but it never reveals the truth of these winding inscriptions, which decorate the frieze, nor will it show them to be paint and plaster, which fritter away in fragments every day.

Ahmad-Ibu-Tooloon, when he chose a Christian

architect to build his mosque, did so with the confessed intention of making it indestructible, and, as an added precaution, he ordered that all the material used in its construction should be of brick or plaster, and, not to take chances, credited his builder with the sum of a million francs for first expenses. From the citadel hill, this oldest Cairo mosque appears somewhat like an immense fortification; the walls are sculptured in trefoil design, like the round towers of England. Abbas Pasha remodelled the superb building into a military hospital, filled in the arches with plaster walls, and broke away the pillars which cost Ahmad a lifelong outlay more than a thousand years ago. To-day the mosque, as an hospital, is shattered and fallen, but the sick of Cairo cling round it still with faith in its miraculous powers; it is the rendezvous of all ills and all miseries.

The Mohammedan loveth marvels; and the curative resources of the old mosque are not more impossible to believe in than the supernatural legends of its construction.

The guide, who persisted in prowling around with his stock in trade of stories well in hand, in spite of withering glances and an evident desire on our part to be left alone, managed to resume from time to time his parrot-like repetitions, explaining proudly that the mosque had been created before the earth; the waters alone covered the earth; and the Creator, navigating the sea, paused on the summit of the kebla, having come to the end of the deep.

It is impossible to discover how the honor of a premundane construction should befall this edifice, but confidence in the story is evident from the amateur steamboats chalked over the walls representing the event.

Another kebla is surrounded by the most distressing cripples in the world, — the lepers; and it is believed to have been consecrated by the prayers of the daughter of Ali, and the sister of Husên and Hasan, the first martyrs of Mohammedan legend.

Passing up and down before the great bronze doors is a continual procession of poor Arabs and fellaheen children, and from these elements were recruited the very first girls' school in Cairo.

It was the Empress Eugenie who put the proud Ismail Pasha to the blush on the occasion of the opening of the Suez Canal. The Khedive, overweeningly confident in his European innovations, was showing New Cairo to the French Queen, who expressed great pleasure in his eccentric constructions, and innocently asked: "But where is the girls' school?" the boasted likeness to Paris having broken down in this particular, amid so much that was modern and European in the plaster sea of yellow palaces.

The next day the Pasha called his Minister of Public Instruction and ordered a palace immediately constructed where the daughters of nobles could obtain an European education; and to lose no time in repairing this very evident rift in his modern lute, Ismail endeavored to open at once a small house for the purpose. It was with heart's sorrow that the Pasha viewed his failure,—not a noble among them would send his daughter to the Khedivial school; and at length, in great indignation, this rich man of modern times conceived the idea of establishing a sort of primary class in the beautiful shadows of the old sanctuary, and compelling the neighboring children to come in literally at the point of a sword, — a sort of Egyptian form of compulsory education,— thus initiating the first girls' school of Cairo, which was gathered together from the lame, halt, and blind in the crowded quarter of the mosque of Tooloon.

It is extraordinary the number of ruined and half-ruined mosques one passes on the way from quaint old Tooloon to the most beautiful buildings in Cairo, the splendid Gami Sultan Hasan at the foot of the citadel near the Place Rumêleh ; this mosque, in its time, will soon be a ruin too,— but better that than a restoration such as has been attempted in many others.

Turning a corner in a rock-cut street, the cupola

and minaret of the mosque of Hasan stand out in royal purples against the lemon, pink, and blue of the sunset. The proportions reflect something of

AN EGYPTIAN ORCHESTRA.

a cathedral, for the interior is simple and pure, the design is cruciform, the four arms of the cross vaulted and pointed, while exquisite arabesque letters interlaced with flowers are cut in the walls with Cufic inscriptions, and the court of the fountains, the lovely ornaments ranged around the tomb, and the interesting capitals of the columns make one wish to stay a week in it.

In the honeycomb capitals which the architects

call pendentives, I believe, numbers of pigeons make their nest, and a spark of color still remains in the decorations which, though faded, nevertheless show forth the old glory of the "superb mosque."

We had to go through some of the oldest quarters, with a dreary monotony of latticed windows, and into a lane more and more winding and irregular, to visit El Burdanese, the little jewel mosque, which has escaped an embalmment between the red covers of the guide-book. You seem to enter one of those Eastern regions which Hafiz loved to describe. Pale bits of blue tiling are let in over the doorways; mosses have sprung up between the disjointed stones of the old gates, and black water stagnates in the fountains; the picturesque houses look best in the shadows of the narrow alleys, and the busy life of Cairo rarely penetrates the half-asleep population of this silent, enchanted place, where among the ruins "the quiet colored end of evening smiles miles on miles."

A solitary sign of life is the picture appearing beneath an archway,— a picture common enough in Cairo,— of a weazened old woman sitting in the open street in front of her poor little house, sorting beans; and of the brown ones she make a *potage* after they have been placed in water, — a simple meal, often eaten by the Egyptians without common salt or other medicaments, for this luxury is so rare among the people that a sign "Vente du sel" is especially displayed as an indication that it may be procured inside the shop.

The sacristan of the mosque, who answered the summons of a bell suspended outside, was in no wise shaken from his anticipations of a fee by scruples against our entrance into the shrine mosque, because there were not enough slippers to distribute among us; but the straw mattings were rolled aside to a dusty corner to ease his conscience and preserve the sanctity of the building against the tread of an unbeliever.

Five hundred years ago, a pious Mohammedan parent erected the lovely chapel for the use of a son who persistently refused to perform his devotions outside his own domain, and was presented by his father with an especial mosque adjoining his palace. It is a charming little tale; and a vague suspicion of the real motives of this exacting youth, who was perhaps more irritated than pleased by the appended sanctuary, does not spoil its old-world flavor. However, the beautiful building remains, in spite of the truth or falsehood of the story,— evidently not a show mosque, so hidden away in the heart of the strange old house, with the grayish bloom of age on the gloomy walls; but still it is a gem in its small way, built from a sweet devotion, all of inlaid ivory panels and gold-suffused ceiling, "for gold means love," the poet says; and the burnished pearl of the pulpit could also be described in the poetic simile of a "sad, slow, silver smile," when the sun-rays touch it, from the stained glass tracings far above in the glowing walls.

Graceful Cufic inscriptions are delicately cut on the smooth surfaces of the panelling which circles the enclosure, and above them are linked the texts, which are also ascriptions. "To God all that is in Heaven and on Earth!" "O perfect One! O healer! O defender!" and bound in the tortoise-shell monograms on the pulpit is the creed of Islam.

The block of the panels is ebony. The rainbow tints are pearl and ivory, and incrusted among the intricate carvings in glorious prismatic colors are the words "Oh, ye who have believed, pray to Him and salute Him!" while from the mosaic glass of the windows honeycombed with tiny openings, the soft light and a faint breeze come in together. The stillness of the place is undisturbed by two women, who come occasionally to pray in the gallery; at other times it is quite deserted, and always twilight and still, while with closed eyes you can listen to the silence of the vanished voices which have prayed here.

"O Angel of the East! One, one, golden look across the waters to this twilight nook; the far, sad waters, Angel, to this nook!"

IN THE FAYÛM.

AFTER all, it was from a casual remark made at a Cairo dinner that we went a-wandering to the Fayûm's ancient patch of green oasis, which resembles an immense leaf drifted out on the Libyan Desert, veined by various canals and stemmed by graceful curves of the Bahr Yusuf (or Canal of Joseph), with its silken current. The upshot of the conversation was that only fifty-seven miles south of Cairo, westward to the low-lying desert which skirts the Nile, there exists an extensive oasis, a sand-surrounded Venice, due to the efforts of the prehistoric Nile to dig out a channel for itself amid the bordering hills. Having encountered a natural depression near these Libyan mountains, the inflowing waters had spread out annually in this sandy rendezvous a deposit of great richness, and in time deepened the marshy borders into a bright clear lake.

A shining light of the days of Amenemhat III. of the twelfth dynasty is responsible for the grand idea of reclaiming this Nile deposit from inundations, and of laying out the fresh land for a watering-place and fashionable resort for Egyptian aristocracy, where the wind would blow clear and soft from the desert, and the people could delight in the blue lake, inexpressibly sweet amid its setting of summer grasses. At length this was done, and they called the place El Fayûm. That it is still an unfamiliar name to tourists who go up and down the Nile without ever having heard of it, is somewhat due to the fact that Cook does not sell tickets, or provide information of its features or its people. Woman's curiosity quickened at the extraordinary prospect of unimagined villages and unfamiliar lakes, which were dotted about freely in the description given in the aforesaid remarks. A fellow-traveller who had exhausted Egypt's favorite stamping-grounds, and was longing for new pyramids to conquer, listened intently, and striving steadily for some time to assimilate the salient characteristics of the description, including lovely palm-fringed lakes, delicious air, wretched hotel, and necessary military escort, succeeded in reconciling these self-warring facts with a suitable regard for personal comfort, and declared that, properly equipped, with letters to high places, and butter and rolls from Shepheard's, we might ourselves venture to gaze on the mud-brick pyramids of Hawara, and even pursue that will-o'-the-wisp of speculation, Lake Mœris itself. In spite of the dinner-party amusing itself with gentle endeavors to dissuade us from our journey, — evoking unknown hardships and alarming escorts, even accusing us of wishing to emulate Empedocles, whose foolhardiness was only rewarded by Etna indignantly casting out his sandal, — before the coffee was served it seemed better sport than ever to our curious minds, and all the next day was spent in procuring available information and the services of a suitable dragoman. Achmet was the fifth who was distrustfully surveyed and questioned; and cased in cheap blue and humble browns, he was judged favorably where the others, glittering in picturesque and brilliant garments, failed. A large lady in an English tourist's dress had this economic marvel up the river, and recommended him in a well-thumbed letter, which he produced, in which his economies of dress were favorably dwelt on; moreover, it seemed he had better notions of promptitude than ordinary, besides knowing all the routes to the Fayûm; his relatives lived there, and he expressed a very tender love for the place, and was familiar in three languages with all its secrets and antiques. This seemed so favorable that our bargain was sealed, and a parting injunction delivered to find two good side-saddles for the excursion. He kissed my hand, made a fine salaam, and walked out still ecstatic and exclamatory of the good care he would take of " my ladies."

Next morning Achmet had the saddles leaning against a tree in front of the hotel, and a portly proprietary sheik was puckering his vicious old face over the rental of his shabby saddles. After testing the girths of several, and examining their stuffing, with a fine contempt for outside appearances, we chose two most lacking in looks, but having the strongest leather to grip the little beasts who would shuffle their hoofs over the vague but fascinating Fayoum. "Can have saddles one franc each lady," finally concluded the sheik; then we started forward through the early morning mist, bumped and rattled through the Place Ezbekīyeh towards the station, with the dragoman, saddles, and provisions piled high on the vacant spaces of the open victoria. The crowd, the shouting, and shrill echoes from impatient travellers at the ticket-office, forced us to remain apart, on the edge of the squatting clusters of white-turbaned sheiks and native women who were guarding their many-colored possessions while awaiting the signal to board the train; and when our native had first cast down a rug bundle from the box, apparently containing his limited wardrobe, and then himself, sufficient gold-pieces were counted out for first-class tickets, and with an unappreciated burst of generosity, funds for a second-class ticket were provided for our servant, who we noticed pocketed the difference in piastres and invested in his accustomed accommodation of an open pen-shaped car; of course he wanted to be with his caste and have a good talk. There is an upheaval of turbans, and a slow movement sets in towards the train; black people, emancipated Soudanese, and Turks advance, waddling under their cumbersome luggage, through dust an inch thick in the railway enclosure, towards the opened gateway; and Achmet, his head sinking forward under the saddles he is carrying, and clutching as many of our personal effects as can be secured by his small brown fists, pushes ahead, while around us press the " anteeka" merchants, sellers of curios, and boyish harlequins who are dispersed by the simple method of being scraped away by upbraiding sweeps of a native policeman's stick. An old Turk stands under a sort of guillotine, where is suspended a bell; he pulls it by a chain; one soft flute-like ring, and we are off.

Since the completion of the railway, a train starts daily from the Bulak-ed-Dakrûr station, and proceeds so leisurely that anywhere one could climb into the carriages without taking the trouble to stop it.

Cairo is all silvery in the morning mist, and we see a magnified caravan crawling in from the desert. A long file of camels and figures trudging along tall and shadow-like in the haze, and two great yellow pyramids, rise out of a sand plateau as if some hurricane had swept them up from the desert, and they had remained petrified in stone. The carriage has no curtains, and the dust sifts through and soon changes the russet leather upholstery to sand-color. We sit facing two sportsmen, who never once glance at the lovely Medum pyramid, which rises against the sky as if cut from a sapphire, and shines like gold against its splendid background; while nearer the splashing waters of the Nile are the huge sakiehs, with their dripping buckets and oozing creaking music.

We reach Wasta at half after ten, and wait an hour for a branch train to creep in from the Fayûm. There are no time-tables after this; the arrivals and departures depend, as far as we can discover, on the wishes of the native locomotive driver. During a halt we made acquaintance with a dozen little Arab children by aid of a few half-piastres, to which we added some Albert biscuit, and tossed an orange to a *petit maître* in a Wasta compromise of two civilized garments, evidently the " petted child of wealthy parents."

At last the train signalled an intention to start, but was held up by the station-master in compliance with our request to have a feather duster applied to the linen covers of the compartment. This was slowly and thoroughly accomplished under our personal supervision. The saddles were mounted therein; then followed the sportsmen's treasures and ourselves, by this time elbowed by a mob of screaming children, — " Lady, give one piastre," and proclaiming with coquettish smiles, "You nice lady, I like you."

We leave Wasta dozing in the shade of a palm-grove, and cross a strip of cultivated land to the village of Abu Radi, beyond which the railway makes a straight line across the desert, greeting the Bedouin encampment *en passant* with a hoarse tenderness from the throttle of the steam-valve. The air which blows fresh and uninterrupted across the wide desert from Alexandria might be a luxury indeed, if one could only have the windows open, but our lungs are filling up with sand in alarming quantities; besides, the inevitable flies of the kind that secrete ophthalmic poison are swarming in, attracted by the luncheon, and are becoming too numerous to be deterred by the vigorous use of fly-flaps. And so the hot noon comes on us, and the bleak chain of Libyan hills, looking so coppery and baked, sparkles in the sunshine, and seems to glow with the love of it. The sand gusts whistle along, breaking the torpid quiet of the dry sand-stretches on either side, and the humming, vibrating heat intensifies the unendingness of that same even sand, broken only when a glittering whirl of it climbs high in folds of foam, to dissolve again into that land which belongs to no one, and is the desert. At Adweh there are a few white mosques, and the cultivated land begins; four women creep out in dark garments from a low-browed hut at the station, holding in their arms dingy babies, with hardly three good eyes among them. They scent the lunch, and make a clamor like the birds who fly in and out of the almond-trees; the chicken bones, however, satisfy both creations. How neglected it all looks! noticing that, we pass around the sickly flowers, whose faces, "burnt blind" in the sun, struggle for elbow-room beside a row of palm-trees, tall and calm above the hum of voices about the station platform. Palms are always inseparable from curves and harmonious slants, or their tufts are waving; who ever tires of the rough bark, the scales all rippling down the trunks, or the endless ranks of outbreaking branches? Half an hour later we have left behind everything which one knew before in Cairo or, indeed, in our conventional lives, and for compensation obtain, among other things, an insight into the ways and manner of life of a gentleman and an officer in the service of the Khedive, acting in the capacity of chief policeman for the Fayûm Province, who lives at Medinet, the capital of the province, in the little low-roofed and pink-washed building across the sand.

On our appearance at the station we were at once taken off to his quarters. The house was a small one; a bare, whitened hall, which is the vertebra of the building, opened on a sand-patch in front and a dried up garden at the back; and here the officer messed with a guardsman sent down from Cairo to learn Arabic, who occupied the white tent in the compound. At the outer side of the hall one little living room was ornamented with pictures cut from the "London Graphic" and "Illustrated News;" the merry sports of a Derby day or the faces of sweet English girls looked down on the lonely lives of these owners of long titles and discouraged hearts. They do their work well for the Government, and try not to think; but the lack of Europeans and civilized customs is gall and wormwood to an exile from Bermuda. It is all like Kipling's stories transferred to Egypt, — the touching details of how they live; the fever, homesickness, and everything. A small Arab boy applied a shoe-brush to our dusty garments, and then lunch was ready in the queer hall, where the table looked cool and fresh with decorations of daisies picked in our honor, and the officers listened eagerly to the bits of Cairo gossip we had to relate, while various dishes were served by a little Soudanese, whom, the captain said, he had bought for thirty-five piastres.

Through the open door we could see the Mudir's[1] house, flying the red crescent; and with a half-cross expression, both officers declared it "ought to be pulled down and 'ours' put up instead, you know."

The Mudir, the Englishmen tell us, is a strange

[1] The chief official in every province is the mudir, or governor, who is assisted by a council, or dîwân, of other officers.

old figure, who is fond of Europeans, and will converse for hours with men who do not know a word of each other's language. I wonder what they talk about. There are no European women in town, it seems, but there is a Greek lady living at Adweh, the station we passed through thirty miles away on the railway, "who is a very good sort," in the officers' opinion; but the companionship of his fellow-man in English clothes is denied them for many lonely months, when no sportsmen come to the Fayoum.

Long before I came here I had imagined the depression of life lived under such conditions, but the colossal loneliness of it was left unpictured until I saw the reality. We tried in vain to gain some antiquarian information, but they evidently had no recourse to these studies to drown ennui. A vague notion existed in their minds that there were some pyramids straight away from Medinet, but the fallen obelisk we had come to see they had not heard of and did not believe it existed. They had been here many years and never heard any one speak of it, but would go and bring one of the native postmasters, who might tell us something if we really wanted to see it; but the captain was not quite clear, and very much mystified that any one should care at all about a broken obelisk half buried in a beanfield. The non-appearance for hours of this official, who had closed up the post-office for an afternoon siesta, made an excuse for staying as long as we could consistently take advantage of the hospitality we were enjoying; and after tea at four, the native appeared, and expressed the same doubt about the shaft, which, however, we knew was somewhere within two miles of this place. Laurence Oliphant wrote of it, and had personal contact with it; and repeating certain phrases which put the matter beyond doubt, all walked over to the inn, our future abiding-place, where the dragoman had preceded our arrival. Half hesitating, yet anxious to prepare the way for our unfavorable impression of the only public house in the town, the captain confessed, as we walked along, in a few words which revealed volumes: "I stood by this morning, and saw your rooms washed out myself." The truth was, he had not only done this, but contributed big bunches of red roses, and ordered suitable blankets and bed-linen; for until our arrival they were unknown in the Fayûm Hotel. The inn was kept by a Greco-Egyptian, who had determined to furnish his house without owing anything to European civilization except the bottles of cheap cognac ranged round the middle hall, through which we entered. There were rows of tables where chess was going on, and the inevitable Oriental pot-pourri of smoke and hasheesh sent its fumes up to our unaccustomed noses through the open centre hall, around which our rooms were ranged. No lady's sitting-room had been indulged in, or ever required, perhaps; and I was puzzled, on receiving the polite attention of a call from the Mudir, while turning over his rather unique *carte-de-visite* of yellow isinglass lettered in white, whether to receive him in the street or the corridor.

A tiny room, flanked on two sides by the public smoking-room of the natives, was the scene of our first acquaintance with the Greco-Egyptian *cuisine* of the inn; and ever afterwards it was relinquished in favor of our own apartment, and the menu then and there abridged to eggs, jam, and tea, with the precious rolls from Shepheard's doled out as sparingly as the grain of the Pilgrims. The Egyptian has no hours, — he eats where he happens to be when he is hungry; and of the three hundred thousand Mussulmans who fling themselves at the foot of Mokattam, it is said that at least two-thirds can live upon "the Korân, Nile water, and soft bread."

Twice a day Achmet mysteriously disappeared; and we supposed he was in the bazaars, investing his piastres in cheese, spoiled olives, and nuts without shells as tid-bits which he could not deny himself.

Early next morning the dragoman was despatched with particular injunctions, in the language he seemed best to comprehend, to find two donkeys, "fort grand et bien tranquil," which latter specification seemed unnecessary, remembering the desiccated frames of the models of anatomy ridden past our door. Under the guidance of mine host, Achmet was able to present two rather good-looking beasts for our inspection, — for we had discovered that his relatives in the Fayûm corresponded to his knowledge of the languages, and were past finding out. He used to ask Seyd, the keenest of the donkey boys, the names of things in Arabic, and then, by means of a sentence begun, continued, and ended in different tongues, tangle up their histories in unscrupulous sputterings.

Strong in the consciousness of antiquarian zeal, and the hope of convincing our late entertainers, we started forth to find the obelisk in our very first excursion about Medinet. The town is of the usual mud-walled character, but has a plan of its own. A broad canal, the Bahr Yusuf, flows through the middle of the town, and radiates into many branches; it is bordered with well-grown palm-trees, and splashing sakieh wheels driven by the water itself are the rare features of this Egyptian landscape. We ride out along the Bahr Yusuf in the direction of the mosque of Kait Bey, a dilapidated building of the usual square pattern, with lovely pointed work outlining the beautiful Moorish arches, reflected down into the water from the tunnel over which it is built. There is another curious and forsaken specimen of mosque, Sofi, with an unintelligible history, which I do not remember so well as I do the withered speci-

MOSQUE OF KAIT BEY.

men of a beadle who piloted us about, in spite of our efforts to understand Achmet's translation of his no doubt legendary information. In the north of the town are the ruins of the ancient town of Crocodilopolis Arsinoe, a polysyllabic legacy which is commendably abridged by the natives to Kôm Fâris, for a reason I am unable to explain, unless the Western love of abbreviation has advanced the advent of electric light and sewing-machines in the Fayûm.

Endeavoring to accomplish an inspired sifting of the legends and history of the Fayûm, the first claim is undoubtedly for the speculation concerning the transformation of the natural Fayûm Lake into the artificially constructed Lake Mœris of the old traveller Herodotus. The past history of the oasis was, on the authority of modern historians, as follows: In prehistoric times the Nile was a much greater river than now, due to the enormous rainfall. The sea which occupied the Nile Valley was then in communication with the Red Sea, and below Wasta the channel of the Nile Valley very much contracted the enormous volume of water, which escaped sideways into the depressed levels of the Libyan Hills and Wâdi Rayân. Mr. R. H. Brown, in his book on Lake Mœris, states that this water would, in finding a channel for itself, "erode laterally or scour down vertically accordingly as the softer material was in one direction or another." Authentic hints follow which show that "the different points of delivery and volume of water contributing to the flow, and the nature of the rock met with in its path would finally determine the form the channel would take at the various stages of its development. Tremendous eddies would be produced by projections of hard rock and contraction of the irregular channels which would lift the material from the bed." So, the upheaval going on and the Nile scouring out its bed, a condition of levels would come about under which there would be an annual inflow during the floods, and an outflow on the floods' subsiding, thus forming a lake.

Amenemhat III. was a mighty hunter, and to him is given the credit of reclaiming the land of the province to "hunt the lion and bring back the crocodile a prisoner," solving the problem by a series of engineering works, about five thousand years ago, by an employment of hydraulic skill which deserves another paragraph from Mr. Brown. The project consisted of engineering works, admitting water into the lake until it attained to a certain height, and then erecting a regulator and banks at some point between Lahun and Hawara to bar the passage of the Bahr Yusuf through the hills, so bringing the waters into control, when it would be safe to commence the occupation of the reclaimed land. A natural Fayûm lake already existed, and from these operations became the artificial Lake Mœris, with its water surface of twenty-seven thousand acres, with the old Crocodilopolis on its fertile margin, and the Labyrinth and Hawara pyramids, whose dimensions surpassed even the enormous regulators on the shores.

In the middle of the lake, moreover, stood two pyramids, rising above the surface fifty fathoms. On the top of each a colossal statue seated on a throne threw down its broad shadows upon the great white waters.

Medinet-el-Fayûm, the ancient Crocodilopolis, is a country village; it is the produce of the country, the cereals and simple peasant supplies, that are sold in the interminably long bazaar which parallels the Canal of Joseph. In spite of the soldiers who mingle with the animated crowd at the bazaars, it is the familiar fellah with his long blue gown, roped in at the waist, and frequently with only a simple brown skull-cap for head-gear, that is carrying on the bargaining with the comfortable-looking merchants, squatting behind their wares, munching the sugar-cane. The women of Medinet are prettier and less savage than the toilers in the country. Many have discarded the traditional veil, and have commenced to dress their locks with long blue grenadine and golden ornaments of fine finish.

Fat black babies, for whom the climate and vegetarian diet have procured a precocious obesity, squat happily in the dirt; and not a small part of the charm of the primitive life of this terrestrial paradise is the fact that not a creature calls "Backsheesh," — a

A BAZAAR BY THE BAHR YUSUF.

word which we discreetly spell, not to put it in their heads: as you would treat a child, do we treat these children of Khemi.

Away to the north we rode, leaving Medinet in a sea of greenery, and our path took us to the mouldering ruins of Crocodilopolis, that had been first called Shed, and was the villa town where the Court of Memphis enjoyed the lake front and its great expanse of water, which was Lake Mœris. No one would have thought that the deep shadowed walls of pointed and rugged outlines, which resemble a

SOME OLD HOUSES, MEDINET.

Swiss glacier of frozen mud, according to ancient testimony were the remains of the very centre of Egyptian splendor.

Diodorus Siculus, writing of the lake, called after its constructor, tells us that after erecting a tomb and two pyramids, one for himself and another for his wife, thus expecting to leave an immortal reputation for his benefactors, the king felt himself justified in encouraging the extravagant tastes of his spouse by granting her the entire revenue of the fisheries for her perfumes and cosmetics; and he records also that they brought in a sum of a talent of silver daily, for there were said to be twenty-two kinds of fish in the lake, and the quantity " taken was so large that the numerous hands engaged in the salt-curing industry could scarcely keep pace with the work."

We wind in and out, now west, now south, for the ruins are divided by irregular squares and silent passages, and the deserted wastes loom up sheer and pathless, while the donkeys gallop so near the edge of the mud gorges on all sides, that a stumble would solve life's problem for a couple of adventurous antiquarians. A good deal of nervous worry was observable on the part of the dragoman, who anxiously scanned the horizon for signs of egress, but scorned the clever Seyd's suggestions, until we concluded we had come unawares on the mazy labyrinth traditionally located in the Fayûm; and only by insisting that Achmet should listen to the native's advice, did we ever succeed in seeing the sun again, by this time suggestively near the desert's distant edge. But we did not mind this, once out on the pleasant green fields of bean and clover; and Achmet having found he knew nothing of the country, Seyd was promoted to go first, and the dragoman, senselessly enraged, followed on his beast in the rear.

The sheik of a small village we passed after that, stood out on a slight eminence in the long sack-like garment of his race, and offered us coffee and the fruits of his garden and a greeting. The "princesses" do not want refreshment, but can he tell us where to find a fallen obelisk? inquired our anxious Achmet, with self-confessed ignorance of anything and everything in his boasted birthplace. First assuring himself that we are not the spies of Brugsch Bey or the Gizeh Museum, we are conducted to a hidden animal pen, and, the straw being pushed aside, a bit of early Egyptian sculpture is uncovered to our gaze and the cow's stare, which has been jealously secreted from antiquarian grasp in the person of Brugsch Bey, who visited these parts two years ago.

Evidently these relics have an unknown value to native eyes, and, still sceptical as to our honest intentions, the sheik looks very much relieved when we pass out and onward.

The remains of a large temple with a pylon discovered by M. Schweinfurth was an unconsidered trifle scarcely noticed, and also some fragmentary heads and hieroglyphic decorations. A shout to a toiling fellah on a steep hill nearly a quarter of a mile away is answered, and in the mood to listen to any one who offers assistance, the return shout declares that this centre of light and learning will volunteer to conduct us to the object of the quest. Although I have never found belief so difficult in my life, there is a wild scamper of ass-flesh in the direction of a very far away field, and soon a little white glimmer appears through the bean-stalks. Fortune has smiled on us in this strange corner of the earth, and the obelisk of Usertesen I., broken in two mighty pieces, is lying before us, half submerged in the cracked and sun-baked earth, which has receded, and shows a deep line of dark against the white sides where the Nile has traced its burial-marks. One look and then another, while the head guardian pulls away the grass, and we trace the writing of the inscriptions, and the royal cartouche of the king who founded its mate at Heliopolis. It must have once been forty-six feet in depth, and, like all others, its summit is rounded. Still we sit wondering how it came here, who brought it; and now neglected and deserted, is it not a fitting gravestone of a fallen Fayûm? and all the while the donkeys wander off into the fresh pasture, and the boys pull the green beans and eat them *au naturel*, displaying a decided preference to imitate Nebuchadnezzar instead of enjoying a taste of the fruits of knowledge.

The gleam of the soft sunset falls on the white flowers of the bean, and a pale streamlet flushes pink and silver among the clustering reeds and rushes. A last lingering look at the great oblong shaft shows the inscriptions literally written in blood; the sun, who loved Usertesen, floods the names and titles of the Lord of Diadems, son of the sun, with a glory of color, which the darkness will extinguish, and keeps bright the granite emblem of its rays, until we are far on our home-coming through the now scarcely visible field-paths.

Near the villages the cattle are slowly moving homeward; the frogs croak, and the mist of the evening rises silently and mysteriously, magnifying the camels in the high-road, and the tall palms are caught up in it and appear in the clouds. The donkeys pick their way as best they can across the grain-fields, stretching away out, as though forever and forever before us; and the lightning flash of their silver-plated shoes, which show at the various jumps, tell us how quickly the little animals are hastening to their supper of sweet clover at Medinet.

A little later we come to Crocodilopolis, where the foxes are supposed to prowl. Certainly it is grewsome; in the almost darkness we do not meet a creature, but, tightening up the girths, give loose reins to the donkeys, and excepting sharp descents on each side, can chronicle no narrow escapes in this unadventurous record.

All the country seems half a dream, and the more enchanting for the absence of sunlight. Even the hated hotel looks cleaner and nicer than ever; I don't know why, unless it is that we have become familiar with it; and, as some one has well said, "the instinctive desire for home, good or bad, definite or provisionary, commands you to love the spot you have known before."

A DAY'S EXCURSION TO HAWARA.

THE donkey-boys, Seyd and Ayed, at seven in the morning were already waiting under the locust-trees of the Fayûm Inn, while the two beasts looked slick and span from the good results of the extra clover we had pleaded for them the night before. The native postmaster, feeling his superiority over the other officials, from the letter of introduction which he kept folded inside his turban, called to see us off; and one might suppose that an extraordinary event was preparing, from the loungers in the street, and the onlookers of the shops who had left their yellow and green merchandise to learn the strange secret of our expedition.

Very much flattered by the excitement we occasioned, and dispensing with the self-effacing tourist belongings, we confided the green umbrellas to balance the basket of ginger ale on Achmet's donkey, and started off in high spirits; especially as the pretty Fayûm lunch-basket contained two small chickens, some fresh Yoosuf Effendis, and boiled eggs, positively proof against the bad cookery of any nation.

The native soldier detailed to accompany the expedition looked very ornamental in blue uniform with gold stars and silver crescents; and his bright new English saddle, hung on a small and tawny Arabian horse, caused no small part of the general business stagnation in Medinet-el-Fayûm.

The escort, although not in the least necessary, gave a sort of *cachet* to the procession, and finally deprived us of at least one Eastern illusion by proving unmistakably that the Arab is a very poor horseman, not in the least graceful, and accomplished only in the art of staying on.

The party moved down beside the canal, and we came unexpectedly on a very pretentious hotel, built ostensibly for future tourists who may elect to pry into the beautiful scenery of the Fayûm and witness this living page of Genesis, when it can be seconded by the invasion of gas and gastronomy. All along the road lay through fertile fields, where the streams of Yusuf Effendi's canal creep or scarcely move at all between the banks of fine blue flowers, the mysotis of Egypt, most splendidly tinted, which fall from the bank above.

The extraordinary fertility of this part of Egypt surpasses everything one can imagine. The clover, for example, is cut three times a year, and reaches

A MEDINET BEAUTY.

a height unknown in the most prolific countries. Scarcely has the grain been harvested when the point of the plough returns to the soil to prepare a new sowing. The earth, moistened by constant irrigation, becomes so softened that the mere scratch of a match serves to rend it; and the instrument for the work is little more than a pointed piece of wood, drawn by a camel or an ass, for the buffalo is too valuable for sakiehs and wells to work the plough. All the fruit-trees and even the olives of Asia were growing in this perfectly new and enchanting landscape and on this first day of March. It was the season of the yellow mustard flowers, — if anything can be said to have a season where vegetation ignores every natural law. The flowers invade the moist spots, and drink up the sweet waters wherever it is the will of the Nile to give it; and a flower drift of blossoms is sailing away on the edge of every wind-swept stream. Still five miles from the Hawara pyramid, one can catch the odor of black coffee and see signs of activity in the tiny native houses as we brush along their walls, and in the greenest of pastures, while work of the type undertaken by the Fellâhîn Ceres in slavery was going on vigorously in the wheat-fields about the mud villages, otherwise drowsily uninteresting. It was churning-day, and at the sun-baked side of every russet hut a lean woman's figure sat apart on the ground, swinging mechanically to and fro the black hide of a goat, tied by his four legs to a rope suspended from the low-browed dwelling, holding the buffalo milk which in about forty minutes becomes the oily butter the natives delight in.

Close to the edge of the desert, there is a shallow stream to be forded. Our donkeys at first refuse and draw back; once safe on the other side, we look back

A FELLÂH BOY.

at our imposing escort, whose steed had developed an unconquerable dislike to going through the water. I remember the donkey-boy's laughter as the Arab grew more nervous and the horse more stubbornly determined to have his own way, turning about abruptly at the water's edge every time his rider approached it, and refusing to be spurred on a step farther. My last sight of the ridiculous spectacle was a view of scrupulously white trousers wading knee-deep in the stream, pulling the horse across by his bridle, — a disgrace to the name cavalryman; and I had ample time to smother my laughter before the quick hoof-beats of his steed sounded on the sand, for we were now far out on the hard and glittering desert girdle of the Fayûm, on the very bed of apocalyptic Mœris, and before us was the pyramid of Hawara, broken brown and gold under the blaze of noon.

The present and past generation of theories concerning Lake Mœris agree in several particulars at least: the lake was in the Fayûm province, the Labyrinth and Pyramid of Hawara occupied places alongside its border, and the purposes it was supposed to accomplish were to " receive part of the Nile water when the river was in flood, to moderate its excesses and return the stored up water to the Nile when its discharges had fallen low in summer, and supplement its deficiencies;" so says a recent engineering work in regard to this subject. Not being an engineer, and having a woman's conservative delight in remotest tradition, I will give the Arab legend of the origin of the ever mysterious Mœris, feeling that it has as much claim to credence as the story related by Herodotus, who, supposing the whole oasis artificially excavated, naturally asked what had been done with the earth dug from such a tremendous pit, and was glibly answered by the ingenious Egyptian that "it was all carried to the Nile and floated away;" the distance to the Nile being thirty-one miles, and the earth computed at fifty billion cubic metres, it would seem as if there were really giants in those days. The Arab romance translated by an American enthusiast is somewhat as follows: —

Now it appears that Joseph, to whom may Allah show mercy and peace, when he was first gentleman of the star chamber and in high esteem with Raiwan, his Sovereign, after spending his seventy years in this high service, became, as it is the fate of High Chancellors in our own time, an object of jealous envy to the highest lights of the Court at Memphis. These, however, ignored the Egyptian Reichstag, and sounded the King himself. "Has not Joseph's knowledge of war policy and social agitations faded with his beauty, and do gray hairs go with sagacity?" And the mighty Ruler said unto them: "Set him a task which shall serve as a test." At that time the Fayûm was called El Hun, or the Marsh, and served as a waste basin for the water of Upper Egypt, which flowed in and out unrestrained; and after much consulting together, the courtiers gave reply to Pharaoh: "Lay the royal commands upon Joseph that he shall divert the water of the Nile from El Hun and drain it, so as to give you a new province and an additional source of revenue." The king joyfully assented, and hit upon a plan to portion his daughter without calling on the exasperated Centre, whose patience as well as palaces were no doubt well-nigh exhausted from the frequent pauper princes who had married royal wives. "Joseph," said he, "I have no estate for my youngest well-beloved daughter, and, the time having arrived for her dot, I would greatly love to have the submerged land of El Hun to serve my royal purpose. It is surrounded by desert, and convenient to the capital; my daughter will thus be independent and protected." "True," responded Joseph; "it shall be done when you wish it, by the aid of Allah." "The sooner the better," said Pharaoh; and workmen having been collected, three great canals were dug, and the water drained. Then the tamarisks and bushes were cut away, so that when the Nile rose and entered the Bahr Yusuf, it flowed to the Fayûm, creating the land which gave birth to the luxurious rose-gardens of half a century ago. The result was pleasing to Rainan, and he said: "How long did it take you to make this wilderness to blossom?" "Seventy days," was the answer. Then Pharaoh turned to his disconcerted courtiers, and said: "Apparently one could not have done it in a thousand days." So was the name changed from El Hun (the Marsh) to El Fayûm (the Land of a Thousand Days), although the cause of its christening should be cautiously inquired into, since it cannot stand any "higher criticism."

We are now cantering past the same sort of low bushes and tamarisk patches which confronted Joseph before the water came which a modern Joseph would now restore. We watch the somewhat ragged Bedouins encamped on the plain, — squatters we would call them, — and wonder what the flocks are fed on, as no pasture-land is in sight. I ask the dragoman, who had not communicated a single fact since early in the day, when he explained some whitewashed shrines on the roadside. "Look, the tombs by the Arabs," which meagre bit of information imparted slight interest to them. In this case no answer was forthcoming; but somewhere I have read that the accommodating camels can live seventeen days without food and twenty-four without water, only betraying their unfed condition by occasional and very human signs of bad temper when in a state of hunger.

We reach Hawara enthusiastic and happy, and at once climb the soft and crumbling pyramid. Until Flinders Petrie came, nothing was known about its builders, arrangement, or date; *débris* had fallen and rubbish accumulated over its secret entrances and exits, until the determined explorer built a palm-thatched hut for himself on the sun-colored soil, cleared and tunnelled away the brick, and making an inspired guess, finally reached the original trap-door passage to the inner chamber, finding there the richest prizes of the twelfth dynasty; the amulets of a noble of the twenty-sixth; and the Roman portrait-panels, whose extraordinarily vivid colors are like those of a newly replenished palette, and so well done that one can never believe or understand that they were the work of a mere country painter of a provincial village; and then the clumsy rag dolls which had been put to sleep with the little Roman babies in the great secret chamber, and the flowers, the wreath of dried sweet flowers, which had adorned the ancient dames, and show what a florist could do then as now, — all these the learned Petrie brought to nineteenth-century daylight, and many other things which the wise men have brought to England.

Many stories are told of the self-denying desert life of this antiquarian anchorite, who was not, however, proof against temptations of the gastronomic order. I especially liked to hear of the semi-barbarous genius who presided over the *cuisine* during the digging. And I remember the story of an improvised menu, and especially a new plat, which, if imitation is the sincerest flattery, might well cause conceit to its inventor. It was a very available dish, — several eggs, first shaken together in a bottle, treated to buffalo milk and butter, then scrambled on a tin sheet over an alcohol lamp, *à la* Petrie, to whom necessity confided the receipt; and its very simplicity enabled us to face every luncheon possibility of future expeditions with perfect serenity.

The lurking savages of the Bedouin encampment gathered in from their brown tents, and I proposed they should go and dig up something, Philistine enough to covet some beads or mummy wrappings. At the rate of four piastres a day, the tariff of Brugsch Bey, they began delightedly; and a few minutes of literal handiwork resulted in scrubbing out a shrunken mummy hand and a yellow skull with dangling black hair, just a little way from our lunching-place. This was too much, and we begged them to stop. It was scarcely cheering, a much too severe test for amateur body-snatchers unfortified by sufficient food. However, the digging went steadily forward until the whole flock had grubbed up enough curios for a museum, whose authenticity, moreover, was not to be gainsaid.

Although the pyramid is the main object at Hawara, it is a lesser light to my mind than the Labyrinth, whose existence had been so faithfully backed up by Herodotus. On the south stretches a wide mass of chips and fragments, associated with and once making part and parcel of this gigantic building; for these mouldering fragments are considered to be the remains of the labyrinthine wonder which the Greeks strangely passed over in their enumeration of the seven marvels of the world, whose foundation stones laid so heavily on my childish brain, in the rigmarole so rigidly learned at school, of which only the pyramids remain in evidence. In a few minutes we had extracted every drop of information contained in Baedeker, and were prowling around among those uninteresting chips of broken pottery; for the stone structure of the Labyrinth is only a crypt for the ruins of a town of brick buildings built on its site. According to the comparisons of guide-book phraseology, the whole Labyrinth must have been in the shape of a horse-shoe, but so vast that all the buildings at Memphis, and the great pyramids themselves, could be contained in its great area.

Imbued with a reckless spirit, and overcoming the inclination to bask lazily in the sunshine, we poked about with umbrellas and crept into the low excavations; but some fragment of capitals in the red stone of Assuân or limestone blocks were the rare and unsensational reward of various trips and falls among the ruins. Of the great single blocks which often formed the ceiling or the floor of the chambers there was nothing to be seen. The old king, we are told, used for the Labyrinth only the granite of the Assuân Hills. Not an inch of despised wood or other material formed these winding halls, with illusive passages running through them, which had a decided family likeness to the modern maze, but of such solid strength that, like the wonderful "one-horse shay," they were warranted not to wear out. Nevertheless a small town of masons once existed here for the pronounced purpose of their destruction; and these moderns, or rather Romans, by a characteristic trick have quarried and mined this immense edifice until not one stone remains on another of those massive works of the ancient artisans. No doubt their indignant ghosts walk by night. The pyramid of burnt Nile bricks at the end of the Labyrinth is the tomb of the former occupant of this vast palace, which consisted of as many royal dwellings as there were magnates, representing different nomes, who assembled there in council in serious times to offer gifts and deliberate on affairs of state. Imagination is so powerful, femininely speaking, that we just feasted our eyes on the unbroken sea of red pottery fragments as though they were the superb achievement of Ismandes himself in all its enormity of enterprise; and feeling that everything had been properly appreciated, we departed amid a loud accompaniment of savage salaams, soon losing sight of Hawara, the Bedouins, and our mimic pyramid of apollinaris bottles lying in the cool shadows of its prototype.

At daylight next day, the weather was all right and the sun was coming up soft and not too brightly over the palm-trees. Attractive as was the rhythmic name of Berket-el-Kurûn, or Lake of the Horns, it would be an adventurous traveller indeed who would risk a sun-stroke on the borders of its green waters, when the proper conditions for such a catastrophe were apparent from the singeing aspect of the coppery sun itself.

A train leaves Medinet once a day for Abuska, bordering on the salt marshes, and stops anywhere you wish as obligingly as a hansom cab. Halts are made frequently, — at various mud-granaries, for instance; occasionally we are held up by friendly Arabs who board the train, or we jump down and pick flowers, or a sportsman sees some game; any or all of these things will serve as an excuse for stopping. But at last we come slowly on Abuska. There is no pretence for a station as yet, but one day it will be there, — flying red awnings and busy book-stalls. The outlines of the lake are inconspicuous in the blue distance; and as we brush back the thick growth from the *débris* of an old sugar-cane factory, from our perch among the rusty boilers we discover a pretentious two-story plaster house with a balcony in contradistinction to the regular Abuska mud dwellings. The director of the railway lives there, no doubt, and for the sake of a good view we are soon walking uninvited into the ghost of a sun-withered garden. We taught the dragoman a little speech, and sent him in to ask permission to view the lake from the house. A moment later he beamed upon us with a satisfied expression, and the information that the sister "by him speak Turkish." I wonder if we have impressed Achmet all this time as Turkish ladies? The characteristic national costume soon appeared, and a wistful face with pathetic black eyes made up for feminine shortcomings in way of red and white paint on cheeks and lips of the "sister." We all went up on the high veranda, and then came coffee and cigarettes, which latter were indulged in by the director, as he smiled compliments and talked broken French, while he fingered his Moslem rosary.

The Libyan hills are pink and lemon over the violet water, and pelicans fly across its sunset colors. All around are sterile banks of mud and sand; and the fishermen, in curious boats without deck or mast, stand on the flooring of the stern, while others are rowing against the wind, for the fish always swim in the same direction. The landing-place, Khashm Kahîl, springing up from a great growth of tamarinds and reedy bushes, stands out on a slight promontory; and the sportsmen who alone have known of the loveliness of the lake have never revealed its beauties, for the tourist's advent would soon spoil the richest game country in the world. Wild geese, gray pelicans, and pink flamingoes swarm to the "nourishing ooze," and a hundred wild fowl, whose names I do not even know, flock about the lake banks. On the other side big game and savage lurk in the desolate cactus hedges and deserted temples under the Libyan mountains; and this is not a mere traveller's tale, although I have carried away many that are.

The young moon shone on us, and a great fanfan of musical instruments greeted our return to Medinet. It was the Melah, and that evening we all went to a native circus. There was the usual great tent, and two chairs were placed for us below the rows of bearded Turks, — "Conscript Fathers," in classic black gowns, who squatted in solemn ranks along the tiers of plank seats, as if ready to pronounce sentence. The situation really recalled a Roman arena; only there was no victim, excepting a nervous camel trained to walk a tight rope. It was past ten o'clock, and the circus had only just commenced.

The absence of tawdry lace and tinsel, of hydra-headed phenomena and freshly arrived Italian equestriennes, made the scene unfamiliar; but the fine Arab athletes were as barbarian as one could desire, and the Egyptian clown, colorless as white paint could make him, was unusually funny without understanding a word of the nonsensical rigmarole he uttered, which, however, did not dispose the Turks to laugh.

We soon left, and wandered through half-lit bazaars. In a cramped corner a group of white-bearded muftis chanted the orisons of Saint Roube, whose birthday gave us the Melah; and all squatting on the dark ground, swaying to and fro, the light of a single lantern hardly prevented our stumbling over them at their devotions; while outside the evening waxed gay, and the music grew louder from little half-dim dens on all sides, for "when the sun sinks, all Africa dances."

A FELLÁHÍN REPAST.

THE CAIRO OF THE MOSLEMS.

WE went yesterday to see the University of El Azhar, which means the "flowery," the greatest centre of Mohammedan learning in the world. The Mohammedans no longer have any spirit, or show any bigotry when the guides take you to see their religious institutions. They have even made the way easy by distributing tickets among the hotels, which may be obtained of the porter at two piastres a mosque. These are collected by the custodian priest at the entrance gateway, but that does not prevent him from announcing frankly that a fee is expected; and one is generally acquiescent, well knowing the demand is simple extortion, but to be humble and submissive under beggars tends to render travelling anywhere easy and endurable.

Everything about the mosque of El Azhar is remarkable. The very entrance is through a street of the Middle Ages, winding between irregular and picturesque groups of houses, with charming originality of outline, and bright strings of chillies festooned over the gateways to ripen in the air. It is by the great west door of the mosque that one enters the long outer corridor which serves as a gathering-place for dealers of all kinds, selling their vegetables or clover; and just outside, in the muddy lanes, are the little dim holes where all the articles which the students may need are made before their very eyes.

The finest cloth fabrics alternate with baked bread and fruits in vinegar. The students pass their time when not in the mosque at the neighboring bookseller's, or barber's, or are snatching a hurried meal from the simmering contents of a brass pot; and you will find the quarter of the University the busiest corner of Cairo, — a great Noah's ark of trade, which combines profit and religion under the shadow of the flowery mosque.

At the outer door of the court, we step on holy ground over a low barrier which divides it from the much cleaner, but more unhallowed world about it; and regarded merely from an artistic standpoint, the first view of the whitewashed walls is disappointing. I recommend its charms only to the antiquarian gormands, — for it is here you can feast on *origines* of Islamism; or if you can love and venerate a stray bit of *débris* from Mediæval Ages, these walls have preserved it pure since the month of Gemasi in the year of the Hegira 359, when they were founded by the Fatimite general, Gohar. We are visiting a university without an endowment, where thousands of students have no dormitory but the mosque, sleeping extended on the pavement of the great court in their light cotton gowns, where no fees are paid for board or tuition, and where the simple meals are eaten in the open colonnades, while the sparrows fly down and pick up the crumbs. Although unable to explain this curious restraint, coffee and tobacco are strictly denied the students, who dine in the commons of the mosque. College lodgings are unnecessary, for the walls are lined, where the doors and windows allow, with rough cases resembling packing-boxes, which contain the students' wardrobes; and their diminutive size would indicate one drawback to the extravagances of western college boys. No terms are catalogued, to be well considered before the luxury of learning is possible. The Administration of the Wakfs, which has charge of all mosques and other religious institutions, makes no demands for fees, but on the contrary sustains the scholars and furnishes them with provisions. To do this, they divide the students into riwaks, or quarters, corresponding to the different countries represented. It is these riwaks which constitute the mediæval peculiarity of the place. You involuntarily think of the old custom of separating foreign students, which survives in the "Latin Quarter" in Paris, and remember this geographical arrangement is only half forgotten in Germany even now. Each riwak of El Azhar has a sheik, who is the head of the company of boys under his command; and over all there is the great Sheik of the university, — the President, as it were, of this Oriental faculty, who is the wiseacre of Egypt, an Oriental Pope in Arab domain, who speaks *ex cathedra* on all religious questions, sits in the chair of Mohammed in the St. Peter's of Mohammedanism, and is the head of a great university, where the learning, though limited and insufficient, is in focus. At least, they have their dogmas better in hand than the followers of Hegel and Schopenhauer, pulling at the bit, and reining up no one knows where; here the creed is simple enough: " Lâ ilâha ill' Allâh."

More than seven thousand students attend the classes; Turks, Nubians from the bookless wilds of Africa, Kurds, natives of India and the holy cities of Mecca and Medina, make the most interesting groups about each white pillar, where a professor is expounding the Korân, commenting on each word separately, and treating the interruptions in the way of questions with great patience.

At the base of these columns, which make a marble forest of the court, a circle of students are ranged, seated in the Arab manner with crossed legs, or crouching on the palm-matted floor. The learners are of all ages and all colors; some are sleeping, some knitting, while others follow attentively the discourse of the teacher, and the number is more or less large according to his reputation. Many are old men, for it is really an agreeable place of sojourn, this free and liberal college; and it must require a certain amount of courage to leave it; besides, it has the honor to remain the one famous seat of wisdom in the Mohammedan world.

The Arabs taught geometry about four hundred years ago in their university; then they found the Korân contained everything necessary to know, and here this very reminiscent theology is taught even the smallest children from seven years old, — girls being admitted to study with their brothers up to the age of ten years. Though some of the little girls are blind, they seem as patient "a range of pupils" as the noble ladies of the Princess Ida. Like them, they press in from the provinces to attain the knowledge which will result in that uplift of their natures,

> "Until the habits of the slave,
> The sins of emptiness, gossip, and spite
> And slander, die."

As a reward for the draught at the unsealed fountain of knowledge, the little Academicians are afterwards permitted to recite the Korân at funerals, a singular compensation, and I doubt if they are consulted.

The shortest and easiest chapters of the Korân are the last in the book; and beginning at the end, the children learn to read, to copy, and to recite it by heart, — a real *tour de force;* but as everything depends on memory in a Mohammedan education, it is like the training for the trapeze, — you cannot begin too young to limber up.

According to the fashion of the country, a rocking motion is constantly kept up by the whole school, — a shaking to and fro, which we are told is meant to keep them from falling asleep. A master in a black gown is engaged in imparting a rudimentary knowledge of the Arab parts of speech to his small audience, who, attentive and quiet, unlike other children, do not seem at all conscious of our presence. A couple of rods, with their ends well sharpened, look very much out of place here where the saying, "Boys will be boys," is untrue.

The children are striving to understand that the noun in Arabic "declines according to its case," and that "all nouns, verbs, and participles are variable." Other teachers are seated on the uneven pavement in like manner, for desks are unknown. A primitive tin slate and quill serves for the writing-lesson; and only the larger boys are recruited for this branch, for their extraordinary language is, as every one knows, as difficult to write as to read, — a sort of short-hand, with the vowels left out, and read from right to left.

Our companion, a Coptic gentleman, who studied at Oxford, tells us the instruction at the older Moslem university is, strangely enough, almost confined to the exegesis of the Korân, the interpretations, and the traditions; that the sciences are unknown, the Mohammedans, with few exceptions, believing that the earth is perfectly flat, that Egypt is the mother of the world, and the sun is held in the sky by a great dragon. The importance of the traditions, called in Arabic "hadîth," is easily accounted for by the treatise of an Arabian savant, containing four thousand different ones; while another compilation consists of more than seven thousand, which are transmitted from doctor to priest with minute exactness, each teacher possessing a number in his memory. These traditions and dogmas date back in a genealogical succession to the disciples of Mohammed; and from that remote day to this, not a shadow of doubt has been brought to bear upon their well-worn phrases. It is impossible to visit a college where the students are more occupied with the ambition to become learned; a singular example of this exists in the conference held by scholars after the lesson, when the most clever among a few intimate friends explains to the dullards the difficult points of the study they have undertaken. It happens sometimes in the mimic school that the teacher finds his vocation, the conference decides his whole existence, and is the point of departure for a brilliant life. The wise and gentle Amiel says: "It is by teaching, that we teach ourselves; by relating, that we observe; by affirming, that we examine;

by showing, that we look; by writing, that we think; and by pumping water, that we drain water into the well."

Nothing succeeds like success. Soon the young savant, in his turn, seats himself under a column; and as unquestioned liberty is allowed to follow a purely elective course of study, the new master, if he has *esprit* and talents, attracts quite a circle of auditors. Then comes the test of wisdom, in the visit of the thirty-one dread sheiks of the college. The faculty proceed to a rigid examination of the aspirant, making an inquisitorial demand on his knowledge of the law and the doctrine, until he either comes forth anathema, and even his disciples mock him, or victorious, and worthy to sit in the seat of the professors, a ready-made sheik of El Azhar.

It is a well-established custom in Cairo that, at every stopping-place, the horses are relieved of their bridles and allowed to munch numberless meals of clover; waiting for this proceeding to be concluded, we had plenty of time to hold a short conversation through the guide with a small girl student, who, from curiosity, had left her lessons and followed us to the street, holding a tin slate covered with beautiful Arabic texts which she had just written. A small coin smoothed the way to its possession, but unfortunately the more bigoted boys had sighted this awful wickedness,— the sale of the holy writing to an unbeliever, — and came screaming up to the carriage holding up wet sponges in each dingy hand. Finding the lady obdurate, a war of words followed, which ended only when, the driver lashing his horses, we started forward and dashed down the street, clutching the slate high in air, the little bigots still shouting and clinging to the steps, finally succeeding in effacing the writing, leaving only black and soapy sponge-sweeps over the now worthless piece of tin; but the little Eve kept her piastre, and looked on, placidly smiling a sweet salaam as we disappeared.

A portion of almost every day we spent wandering in and out of a part of the four hundred mosques of Cairo. They take up a great space in every street; their domes and minarets combine with other graceful forms to make a part of every picture. Still they all are very nearly alike, new and old tinted gray or maize, the Egyptian color of mourning, and all have fallen into a picturesque decay. The interiors are generally sown with rugs, and are simple and quiet, with no ornaments except the rich carvings of the Korân inscriptions, and the intricate arabesques of red and gold paint. Near the noisy bazaar of the copper-smiths, and close by the ruins of Es-Salah, which fell a few years ago, is the superb old Muristan of Kalaûn, with its beautiful bronze gates. The floor of the entire mosque is inlaid in colored marble, a linking pattern of keys spread over its walls, and the Kibla, or niche which looks towards Mecca, adds an aimless design of exquisite pearl-work, the model of Hatoon's workmen in the Mousky. In the centre, four old Byzantine columns support the central dome, and the corridors are vaulted in a Gothic design. A doorway leads to the tomb of the Sultan Kalaûn, which is now an office for the Wakf administrators, who, since they cannot sell the church properties, but may exchange them, allow the mosques to fall into decay and ruin. Once the Muristan contained a separate ward for every known disease; and connected with it was a dispensary and lecture-room for students, — a sort of clinic; and everything was free, and the poor and rich fared alike. A sick man lies rolled in a black heap; he has crawled in from the world outside, and lies unmolested on a frayed rug in the cool shadows of the pillars. The hospital has disappeared, but the columns possess a miraculous power over disease; and they are always sticky from the limes rubbed over the worn surface, polished like glass by constant rubbing. The lime after touching the pillar is placed to the lips, and instead of healing, might often become a means of contracting a disease.

The guide thinks a surer way is to lick the stone itself, and shows how it is done. There is only a crumbling wall between us and a shouting, yelling, pushing public. You can hear the rush and roar outside, the shrill cries of pedlers, and the hammering of the copper-smiths; but the approaches to the mosque are by a courtyard, and the crowd cannot enter except in this way to disturb the worship within.

A second great building, the fourteenth-century mosque of Barkûk, stands opposite, with a graceful minaret and some lovely traceried windows. A great bronze door leads into the bright marble-paved vestibule and vaulted passage. The door itself is gigantic for the proportions of the building, but the knocker rises more than twelve feet above the floor. The guide cleared up the mystery to his own satisfaction by saying that in Adam's time men were taller than now; and the dust of centuries, which has collected about the half-ruined arches, would seem to indicate an almost prehistoric foundation.

In the centre of the court is the Mêda, or Hanafîyeh, where the faithful bathe before prayer; the drinking fountain has an unclean and unsanitary look.

We pass under a doorway into a sort of chapel shrine; it is the tomb of Sultan Barkûk's daughter. The place is almost inaccessible, from rubbish; great pieces of colored marble are falling off in places, and cracks admit the daylight and the noise together. But it is thoroughly Cairene and Oriental, and, like everything else in Egypt, picturesque. Going out, an inscription in rich gilt breaks the general gloom of the place. We ask the guide what it all means; but he shakes his head, the shrewd fellow, and hides his neglected education by saying that it would be a sin for a Mussulman to repeat any verse from the Korân to a Christian. I intend to write nothing about the splendors of the mosque El Ghûre, whose beautiful entrance is one of the best remaining in Cairo, or the little Abû-Berk-ibn-mizheh near the blind school, and a dozen more. There is nothing to tell that the guide-books would not make plainer, and I can only break my determination for Mohammed Ali, the Mosque of the Citadel, and for the sake of its great dome. This building, for which no one has a good word to say, is built on the plan of St. Sophia at Constantinople, with lemon-colored blocks of alabaster incrusted in its masonry, and in the sunshine it seems a great bright mountain. You can overlook the ball-room effect produced by the gay ornaments and red and gold decorations, and forgive the operatic glitter of globes, each with its candle, which rain down in circles from the high ceiling, and tinkle when the wind blows from the open door first high and clear, and then dying away softly. All this is in the worst possible taste for a basilica, which it so nearly resembles; but the great dome is so vast and uplifting that you

THE CITADEL.

scarcely notice the gaudy modern rugs which carpet this mosque seven deep, or remember the unattuned pavilion in Chinese pattern in the court, or the incongruous French clock presented by Louis Philippe. The citadel built round its base is a huge stone mass reared by Saladin, in 1166, from the pyramid quarries at Gizeh. It has all the quaintness and mediæval spirit about it which the alabaster mosque cannot claim. Old and shrunken and lustreless, it seems even plainer and more gloomy as you leave the gorgeous modern mosque, and pass through the winding and crooked lanes cut in the rock itself and into the inner gate of the fortress, on the hill which was chosen, according to tradition, from the fact that provisions would last here twice as long as in any other place in Cairo.

From the wall of the citadel we look down on the gray and white town below us, and away to the vivid green of fertile land, watered by the Nile, which borders the yellow desert and the distant pyramids.

This view of Cairo is certainly one of the most interesting in the world. The fortress is now the barracks of British soldiers; the Black Watch of Edinburgh is quartered there, and the owners of plaid tartans are as thick as a Scotch mist on the overhanging balconies. Driving away from the citadel, we pass a ruin called the new mosque, now abandoned, it is said, for the sole benefit of the army of occupation, because, if built, it would destroy the range of English guns, when firing from the fortress into the city in case of any little insubordination among the Egyptians. Most Europeans wrongly suppose the English are there to protect the Khedive's authority, and that his people are the rightful owners of the land.

A SCHOOL NEAR THE MOSQUE.

A SHEIK'S HOUSE.

IT is not a difficult thing to accomplish the renascence of the personages of the Mamelukes. Here are their palaces, where so many tragic dramas were unfolded, and the narrow streets, curving and overhung with balconies of carved wood, which remain perfect pictures of mediæval grace and beauty. The doorways, leading through thick stone walls of this old quarter, are scrolled and twisted with arabesque fret-work; garden glimpses of terraces and fruit blossoms rise beyond the stone steps, and a Lazarus is always at the gate.

The dust need not be shaken off the history of four hundred years ago in Egypt. The scenic effects of that time have hardly changed; and even the decorations of the tombs, fresh with warm colors, evoke the images of the men who sleep, and rekindle their deeds. The exquisite and imaginative mosques which extend far along the east side of Cairo are known as the tombs of the Mamelukes. Nothing could be imagined more delicately beautiful, more fantastic and graceful. One is filled with wonder at the infinite variety of the minarets, the brilliant confusion of colorings, the fretted windows, and faded, incrusted woodwork of the interiors, whose interlacing stones are brightened by softened rays from jewelled windows.

In front of us, from the windmill hill, rises the mosque tomb of Sultan Barkûk, not big or gloomy, but smiling and sparkling with two flower-like domes rising impartially over the tombs of the male and female portions of the family in a way which a woman suffragist might approve. At sunset, the rays inundate the minarets and cupolas with rose and gold reflections. The gray and pink cube of granite which is the mosque of Kait Bey takes the flame colors which flood the mountain background; and, viewed from the hill, the details of plaster lace-work, bronze and marble decorations turn all violet; the blue Nile flecked with white sails loses itself in the distant trees of Shubra, while the tones of the desert, sweeping up to meet the glow of sunset, seem a fusion of molten glass.

The old quarter of the Mamelukes lies close behind the Mousky; and when you have passed under the gateway, remember you have gone backwards four hundred years, into the gray past of palaces now crumbling, pallid, and tottering on feeble foundations.

The end of a block often closes the perspective in these militant and luckless streets, for the mediæval gentlemen fought one another *ad libitum* behind their thick stone walls, and curved and twisted the approaches to them with a view to prevent the insurgents massing their forces. There is hardly room for two carriages to pass, and all pedestrians are forced against the gray walls on either side. One can study the buildings conveniently only where they cut the sky-line, since the attitude of star-gazing alone brings in view their upper stories above the high walls.

In the heart of the shadowy streets, sunk between strong walled houses and dying out in narrow lanes, choked with fallen and crumbling blocks of stone, you see the boundary lines of a palace, spreading around a great hollow square.

A young Mohammedan, with full, calm face, almond-eyed us as we approached the wooden bench where he was seated, talking most familiarly with attendant Arabs. This personage in a sacred green turban of enormous dimensions towering above his copper-colored complexion represents the family of Mohammed, and is the Sheik Abdul Kareem Sadad, the greatest dignity of Moslem society, although he did not seem to take his vocation very seriously, or even to maintain the least appearance of saintly demeanor before his retainers, who, with the usual sprinkling of beggars, were smoking in a very democratic manner, and the man who seemed most to enjoy the occasion was the wearer of the ermine-lined mantle, which opened to show a loose silk tunic flowing out over the board bench at the gateway.

The remark has sometimes been made, that people all over the world of the same calling resemble one another. The head of Clan Mohammed would be recognized anywhere as an illustration of the comfortable leisure class, accustomed to privileged saintliness, and a dictatorship in ideas and customs. A visiting-card was handed to the young Sheik, who, knowing the name engraved on it, at once begged us to enter, and as we say Salamate, we leave him still puffing outside, like the heroes of the "Arabian Nights," while a servant is detailed to show the house. The truth in this case costs an immense moral effort; the renouncement of the Sheik's personal attentions to this part of the hospitality was most unflattering. It would have been such a pleasure and satisfaction to have accepted the services of the real son of the Prophet in introducing the ladies of the house. However, the occasion proved interesting enough. We followed the attendant through an arched gateway, where he slipped off his yellow morocco slippers, and motioned us through the nearest door. A fantastic, but noble structure rose in the dry sunlight of the courtyard. The walls were gray and old, and in some places the mushrebîyeh screens had cracked off, and the harem apartment lay half open to view. The rents in walls and casements were places for sprays of grasses to hang from; and out of the central court grew a splendid tree, as old as the house itself, — that is, four hundred years.

The great court was quiet as the grave; two low, unpainted benches with high arms were unoccupied, and showed signs of dissolution, like everything else. A balcony sprang out of the mud-covered walls, with bird-cage projections, carved in dice-like blocks and gray like the rest, a stone spectre of the Middle Ages itself.

The bright, warm sun-rays shot into the blackness of a great empty room, as the inlaid door swung back; and we felt as though we had been transported through the ivory gate by which all good dreams come. This beautiful apartment of state is a peacock room, and like nothing else but itself and the bird's plumage. Old Persian tiles of blue and green glaze line the side walls, meeting the beautiful arabesque ceiling, which drops down at irregular places in a painted shower of spangled stars carved in wood. Where the tiles have fallen away, coarse pigments have carried out the effect in the same colors. Not a European shade or tone is anywhere to be seen.

Niches hold pyramids of artificial flowers, dusty and unreal; and great glass chandeliers with green crystal tears swing from the starry canopy of the ceiling.

Another high-walled room, with the same soft coloring, opens from the state apartment; there are no violent contrasts in this harmonious old palace. In this room are kept the Sheik's silver-and-green robes, and his state turban, crumbling away in an enormous flowered bandbox, from which the servant drew it tenderly, and with great care, declaring it to be two hundred years old, — a very truthful comment, judging from the destruction accomplished by the moths.

A foretaste of one of the principal joys of a Mohammedan Paradise is enjoyed by the wearer of the emerald robes, for the Korân promises, "As to those who believe and do good works, we will not suffer the reward of him to perish; for them are prepared gardens of eternal abode, which shall be watered by rivers; they shall be adorned therein with bracelets of fine gold, and shall be clothed in garments of fine silk and brocades; reposing themselves therein on thrones."

In this room are shown the portraits of the more or less civilized ancestors of the house of es-Sadad, — aristocratic, high-bred Mohammedans, whose day was in the long ago, in the time of barbaric trappings.

Wealth and children the Korân states are an ornament to this present life, but adds that "good works which are permanent are better;" however, one would certainly conclude, from the contrary impression obtained from the innumerable portraits of the sons and daughters hanging on the walls, that the opposite direction had been carried out, especially as the immediate ancestor of the present representative is now in disgrace, having been called to account for the disappearance of a retainer with whom he had quarrelled.

At one end of this bright Oriental room, hopelessly out of tone with the preparations for the fast of Ramadan going on about it, and in close proximity to the dusty relics of faithful Moslems, you notice with astonishment the familiar stare of a telephone's open mouth-piece, looking perfectly unreconciled and unresponsive to the dull lifelessness of its surroundings. I carried away with me the delicious aroma of choice cigarettes, which were handed by the servant, of no well-known brand, however, but far finer because grown from the Sheik's famous plantation and for his sole use. These heralded the fruits and coffee.

It was more amusing to sit outside in the garden of oleanders, while consuming Turkish coffee from Persian cups in filigree covers; and the delicious compound, soft as Burgundy in flavor, is a luxury most of all when taken in the orange gardens, or where a wild jessamine's gigantic branch flowers in and out of the lattice screens and hides the crumbling walls to which it clings.

The dwelling-houses of the Mohammedans have rarely more than two stories. Land in Egypt is not dear, and one can afford to spread out his habitation over it, instead of piercing the sky. But what gives the greatest charm to them is that they have borrowed the effect of the atmosphere, and seem to have grown into the landscape, rather than have been built into it.

The principal rooms of an Eastern house look into the garden, or court, especially those of the harem. Usually the windows overhanging the street are placed very high, and barred with iron, while the upper ones jut out onto the street and are screened with endless ranks of mushrebîyeh work. The entrance door is generally quite uninviting of aspect, low and ugly; and behind it is the mastaba, the seat of the door-keeper, while in order to prevent the curious passer-by from viewing the court, the passage leading to it from the street is built in the form of an angle. How one's lungs breathe in the garden-scents, once inside this mysterious courtyard! How cool and fresh the vapors of the moist fruit of dates, grapes, and pomegranates! Flowers grow here as they do in other places; but new kinds of great yellow-colored things greeted us from trees of beautiful foliage. From the centre of the garden, a great tree grows to spread shade over the whole enclosure, — quite a mammoth in its way, if not equal to the Korân tree of Tuba, which fable tells us is so large that a person mounted on the swiftest horse would not be able to gallop from one end of its shade to the other in a hundred years. Concerning this remarkable tree, the prototype of our more normal specimens, which are planted in every Mohammedan garden, the Korân relates that a branch of it will reach from Paradise to the house of every true believer, and that it will bear fruits of astonishing beauty and size, and of tastes unknown to mortal men. So that if any man desire to eat the fruit, it will immediately be presented to him, or if he prefers to sup more substantially, flesh of birds will be served ready dressed. As an added attraction of the bountiful Tuba, it will spontaneously bend down to the hand of any person who will gather of its fruit, and moreover supply the blessed not only with beasts to ride on, ready saddled and bridled, but adorned with beautiful trappings, which will burst from its fruits like Cinderella's carriage from the pumpkin.

An earthly Paradise would be decidedly lacking to an Eastern mind without a fountain, and indeed the principal ornaments of the Mohammedan Jannatal Naim, or celestial garden of pleasure, are the springs and fountains, whose pebbles are rubies and emeralds, their earth of camphire and their beds of musk, — so the saffron-sided Salsabil fountain is typified in the Sheik es-Sadad's well of Nile water, which answers the purpose of washing very well, but unfortunately has not been allowed to acquaint itself with the filtering processes of the stream of Paradise, and is brackish and suggestive of faded ash-color.

The mandara, or reception-room, is paved with mosaic, and the more elevated sides, called the liwan, are covered on fête-days with beautiful stuffs and mats of old Persian colors. Here all native visitors leave their shoes; but the superior Europeans put on, over theirs, ridiculously large yellow slippers, tied so insecurely that they shuffle upon the floors in a way that can only be described as slip-shod.

The liwân is sometimes resplendent with Eastern porcelain and crystal; but often the picturesque hangings are shabby, frayed, and sometimes have vanished altogether, while cheap European fabrications have the places of the originals.

It was during the inspection of the woman's apartment that the true condition of the lights of the harem dawned on us. The principal part of the house reserved for them is entered from the court by the Bâb-el-Harim, and from the unattractive surroundings, the deficiencies of opportunities for education or improvement, the uninviting look of the furniture, and positive lack of comforts, one takes away a very melancholy idea of their lot.

The garden where flows springs of water is there, to be sure, a very Paradise itself to an Eastern mind;

and the Korân holds out little hope to Mohammedan fair ones of their ever enjoying a nearer view of this blest abode.

Far beyond the harem gardens are the groves where ripe oranges drop to the ground, but the women cannot touch them, only look, Tantalus-like, on their golden beauty. But then, women have no souls; no Paradise awaits them; no angel Israfil will delight their ears with songs or harmonies of tingling bells sounded from the tree-tops. Even the really feminine pleasure of gazing on golden-bodied trees, whose fruits are emeralds and pearls, is reserved for masculine eyes.

I have ascertained this definitely from the revelations of the Korân, and it explains why the Mohammedans never indulge in any sentimental ideas concerning their wives; they cannot belie their religion. No doubt the women treasure a vague idea of the comfortable tranquillity of a future abode somewhere, even if the pleasures of it are more sparingly meted out than to their lords, and the Prophet Mohammed seems to have shared this belief himself; admitting, as a compensation for banishment from the highest heaven, the beautified females in their lesser Eden would at least be exempt from wrinkled ugliness, and evermore be young and fair. This was his answer in denying to an old woman the entrance into Paradise. To the feast of the blessed, the commentators admit four perfect women, according to the Prophet. "That among men there had been many perfect, but no more than four of the other sex had attained perfection; to wit: Asia, the wife of Pharaoh; Mary, the daughter of Iman; Khadah, the daughter of the Prophet's first wife; and Fatima, the daughter of Mohammed, for did not even the consorts of Noah and Lot deceive their husbands, and therefore the righteousness of even these good men is not available for them at the last day." So the spiritualistic state of the unhappy females affects even their mundane existence. Many advanced men among these Egyptians, it is true, attempt to overthrow tradition in the treatment of their wives, have even attempted afternoon tea, and allowed them to appear unveiled on the Shubra drive. But the popular indignation was too great, and the gauze was returned folded thicker than before; the ornaments carefully hidden, as directed by revelation, for the Korân repeats the admonition of Isaiah to the women of Judea against the sin of tinkling foot ornaments: "Let them not make a noise with their feet, that their ornaments which they hide may thereby be discovered," says the chapter entitled Light revealed at Medina, and declared in its opening sentence to be a Sura sent down from heaven,—a distinction which other chapters, on more vital topics than bracelets, do not even venture to claim.

Mohammed was inspired also in regard to other articles of feminine vanity. A true believer is called upon to renounce not only the display of shaking rings which Eastern women wear about their ankles, but their jewels, clothes, and the trifles considered dear to a woman's heart. However, the self-denial caused by the restrictions of her attraction to every one except her husband is one that every Eastern woman is well used to making. Every one is familiar with the distressing details of the smothered existence of Oriental womanhood. Many writers have cast a noonday glare of light on it, and the traditions of antiquity are beginning to cower under that unsparing sun of criticism. The wrinkled and hoary notions of the old days will fall to pieces; and the worship of misty antiquity, which has kept dumb multitudes of the world's elder daughters, has commenced to disappear under the clearing-up effect of trade and enterprise, and a good deal of reverence went out of it the day railroads came to Cairo.

The head of the house of es-Sadad was still seated cross-legged on his bench outside his delicious old domicile when we nodded "good-bye," and said something about the pleasure of the entertainment he had given us, in fulfilment of an idea that the occasion demanded something of the kind, although this mode of hospitality by proxy was unknown before, and one was painfully conscious of Hamlet choosing of his own accord to be left out of the spectacle we had witnessed.

Entering the carriage, some one expressed the conventional wish to see the house again; and as we drove off, the Sheik's voice followed us with a puff of smoke, as he threw away the end of his cigarette: "Inshallah," meaning, "If God wills." Was it irony or piety, we wonder.

SHEPHEARD'S HOTEL.

WITH COOK AT SAKKARA.

BESIDE the red marble slabs decorated with golden characters which denote that Thomas Cook & Son have conquered tourist Egypt, appeared, one February morning, a large placard in very plain English, which informed the traveller who passed by, that "An excursion personally conducted will leave Kasr-en-Nil at nine o'clock, February 22nd, for Sakkara and ancient Memphis; tickets fifteen shillings; obtained inside." As the result of this announcement, one is rudely awakened from one's dreams on the morning above mentioned by a tinkling which proceeds from the neighboring electric bells, as if dozens of alarm-clocks had sounded at the same moment. They announce to the waiter at the end of the hall the desire of the inmates of certain numbers to have their tea and toast served in their rooms at once; and it means that fifty have accepted the invitation to the excursion. Cook owns Egypt, is the assertion of every traveller one meets *en route*, — who then describes how implicitly the Khedive has confided to him the river Nile, where the red flag of Thomas Cook streams from a perfect flotilla of side-wheelers, and even flirts from the mail-boats despatched to the second cataract and beyond. He excavates the ancient tombs, and has no rivals in the field of hotels. The natives recognize this, and when asked the best inn to be had in a place, immediately answer, "Cook's," which often turns out to be the property of some enterprising Italian, is called the Victoria, and is only recommended in the guide-book of the great Sheik of the tourists. Do not the sightseers gather before him and listen to his wisdom before departing to traverse the sand wastes of Petrea; and is he not the well-spring of learning concerning "arrangements for the Holy Land," as it is called in the printed circulars thrown throughout the streets like theatre-bills in the Bowery? "My dear sir," he would blandly reply to this flattery, "for more than fifty years have I not made investigations concerning this strange creature, the tourist? Have I not given special attention to his mental capacity, wants, and caprices; and as a result should I not enjoy the adulation as well as the offerings of my beneficiaries, and should not the hieroglyphics over my own doorway recount to the Egyptians my honors and power?" The Kasr-en-Nil landing-place is westward through the European quarter for about one mile, and by a flight of stone steps you descend to the river from the embankment. Here I saw the little steamboat ready for the excursion; and at the same moment the usual

WITH COOK AT SAKKARA. 131

hoarse cries and screams for backsheesh preluded the claims of the ragged wharf population, one of whom tore the reed-cage containing the lunch from our hands, and vanished towards the boat, where the boy and it turned up safely by a miracle, a few moments after. "Rameses II." and "III." were lying near by, their decks being well cleaned by men with hard wood fastened to their feet, and swinging to and fro in time to the chanted Korân; and a dozen of the great man's servants, dressed in blue Salvation Army jerseys, with Cook & Son across the breast in red letters, leaned far out on their long poles, ready to push the "Queen Hatasu" in the stream. I remember also seeing the graceful sweep of a dahabîyeh with two furled sails, and the decks a garden of flowery plants and pretty awnings; a light and airy boat, half spectral, which, once the sails were set, would almost float in air. Returning towards evening in the calm, clear sunset, we met this same dahabîyeh ignominiously towed by a sputtering little steam-tug, whose black smoke curled ironically between the sails, and mocked them.

On deck, linen camp-chairs and a red-covered table occupied the open space under a colored bas-relief portrait of the red-skinned Queen Hatasu in a kneeling position, with her rather critical nose slightly disposed to curl at the moment it was sketched by the court painter to the royal family of the ancient dynasty.

The steamer puffed, drew a long and deep breath at her vapory tubes, and proceeded at about six miles an hour up the river. Thereon followed the gray and sombre dwelling-places of old Cairo, spreading out under the morning cloud-flaked sky. Dense groups of decaying houses, tinted by the same color of dissolution, skirt the river-bank, rising far above the muddy water, seeming the ghost of a town, bewitched into an outward aspect of tumbling ruins, the mummy of Cairo in a faded winding-sheet.

Farther on is the warm bright island of Roda, with the fig-trees and green clover patches growing so luxuriously between the brick walls of a sugar factory, its tall chimney rising over the spot where the Hebrew woman once laid her baby boy among the rushes by the river-side at the sheltered spot where the royal daughter of Rameses would surely come to perform the sacred ablutions with the rising of the Nile; and this child was called Moses in the Egyptian, from his rescue from the waters, and the old, familiar story, followed out in the sacred history, shows him to be in his turn the rescuer of his people.

The river winds, twists, and curves through the palm groves, the steep side-banks showing the rich black soil which will be flooded again next autumn by the rising river. All the way is the accompanying range of gray mountains, called Mokattam; starting up behind the wind-mill hills, and from the steamer deck, we can see the black patches in their sides, which are really huge entrances excavated by the pyramid-builders from these old quarries of everlasting hills, to which the oldest pyramid is only a shadowy and reflected imitation.

The dragoman explains that modern Egyptians merely honeycomb the hills in getting out stone for building, not courageous enough to penetrate where the ancients sunk their dismal shaft into the stony heart of the mountain. There is one chief point on which your eye constantly lingers, and returns to it again: the stony apparition of two slender minarets piercing the sky background apparently half as high as the mountain, from which rises the alabaster mosque of Mohammed Ali, the amazing loveliness of which must be passed over in silence.

Beyond the undistinguished grayness of Cairo, we follow at no great distance a belt of green clover, spangled with yellow flowers, — yellow only for want of a more brilliant word; the brightest sun-dipped coloring I have ever seen was the green and gold of the narrow strip of irrigated border-land between the Mokattam hills and the desert of the pyramids. "Where the water is, there is life," for here, stretching out on both sides of the river-bed, the whole country is like a garden: the felláhîn have merely to prick the soil, when grass and grain cover the earth, and the long-eared buffalo cows almost bury their mud-colored selves in tall clover, which the camels crunch and the donkeys munch in felicity and content. Harvesting and planting are going on simultaneously; and the gravest of laboring people in the world walk solemnly in advance of their string of camels, carrying the sweet grass to the market of the Nile, and oxen hoofs shuffle blindfolded around the well-trodden circuit of the sakieh wheel, bringing up the water in pottery jars to pour out into one of the little canals which irrigate the precious acres of the Nile delta.

Here you can look across the whole of Egypt, or rather that part which the Nile has claimed from the desert, and has spread out along its silvery shining track. "Egypt is a present from the Nile," said the old historian Herodotus; a gift of verdure six miles wide, sprinkled with groves running along the sand-waved desert, which is always to be seen, even in the widest parts. Here grows the lentil, the seductive fruit which lost Esau his birthright; wheat, maize, and every crop in turn is grown according to the most favorable period for cultivation. Moored below this embankment were a forest of masts, seeming like the slanting palm-trunks without the upper tufts of leaves; and out on the river, a flight of swallows seemed to steal down towards us, for the watercrafts had opened their wings, one on each side, and were flying before the wind, and in the distance a single dahabîeyeh resembled a large tailless kite, dragging itself along the water. I looked mystified and wonderingly at the river, the only thing that had not changed from the beginning, of which one could say, Before the pyramids were here; the yellow Nile of the hieroglyphics, the same Nile pictured in serpentine symbol on the inscribed garments of the ancient statues, variously colored yellow or red, as it typifies the overflow or the subsidence of its waters.

A modern sugar-mill, which mashes the succulent cane, stands on a conspicuous site; the natives, however, prefer a pair of hollow sticks, and cane is still sold in a stack or great bundle in the native bazaars. In about two hours we sight a barge improvised as a laundry place, and a little later we arrive at the wharf; at the same time a train from Cairo reaches an unimportant sand-bank, at the village station, where passengers who selected the railway journey dismount near a Jewish burial-ground. This is Bedrashên; and the keen English rector who is conducting a party of feminines on a tour of the East counts his flock and rushes off to be the first to secure the good donkeys for Sakkara. I don't believe he was ordained for this purpose. The impatient asses on the banks, which have been sent from Cairo to supply the excursion, have hollowed out the sand with their kicking hoofs, and are busily sprinkling it broadcast about the place.

After many varied changes and dislodgements, the lambs of the rector's fold at last learn the knack of sticking to an unresponsive donkey; and, divested of all *impedimenta* in the way of umbrellas and books, we gallop off.

The scene is strikingly reminiscent of a carnival; so incongruous and inconsistent are the displays of English ulsters, suitable only for cold European climates, and pith helmets, designed to shelter a guardsman from an Indian sun. A few knickerbockers disport themselves over the desert, and a tramping costume made for the Highland Moors, with heavy shooting boots intended for wading the bogs, moves over the sand astride an Oriental ass. A fairly correct enumeration of inappropriate tourist outfits would be amusing, but lengthy. The "Egyptian Gazette" published, during the winter, an account of a grotesque Mardi Gras procession, which included a representation of the British tourist as he appears in the Orient. The matter was taken up by a firm of tourist agents in Cairo, who complained fiercely of the grievance in that their name had been made use of in connection with a burlesque of their valuable *clientèle*. The affair, after a long and bitter newspaper correspondence, was settled by the explanation that the name adopted by the Alexandrian merry-makers was not really that of a well-known firm, though it so nearly resembled it as to easily deceive the public.

Egypt owes so much to her travellers that she can hardly afford to guy them or their eccentricities. She is said to love them as she does her quails, and even sorrows at the departure of those who think " Cairo would be a delightful city were it not for those tiresome temples and those horrid tombs."

There are several different routes from Bedrashên to Sakkara; one of these leads past the site of Memphis, and is used for the winter period, when there is no inundation. As we ride along, not a vestige of imperial or legendary glory can be seen on the dull sand waste, strewn with broken fragments of pottery, and granite blocks.

A solitary statue of Rameses II. lies in a mud-caked hollow, its massive face turned to the earth; twice a year the Nile bathes it, whereupon the features and limbs are gradually destroyed, and the cut of the raiment altered. A mud wall surrounds the statue; and a showman from Cook's mounts the little platform built over the mighty fallen one, and tells you that, when erected, this statue stood alone in front of the temple of Ptah at Memphis; points out the beard artificially attached to the chin, and estimates the measurement before injury to have been forty-two feet in height. At one time the colossal antiquity was presented to England by the descendants of this same Rameses. Strangely enough, the authorities of that wise little island refused it; perhaps they fear the Greeks even when bearing gifts.

An Arab boy was left in charge of the donkeys, which grazed on the fresh grass while the tourists were engaged in cutting out initial memorials of themselves on the wooden platform above the famous barbarian.

A short distance from the statue, half hidden among the shady palm-trees, I discovered a sandstone something, — an important-looking foot, which possessed neither guide or conductor to recount its ancient memories, like similar and more fortunate remains.

There was no one but the donkey boy to appeal to; and nothing daunted by the unexpected demand on his dynastic knowledge, he replied in an off-hand manner, "Some more Rameses the Great;" and I agreed with a smile, for who could venture to deny it?

Forty minutes more brings us to the outskirts of the desert; and the way ascends to a plateau over the ruins of an ancient town, once inhabited by the embalmers of the dead. Mariette Bey's house still stands close to the entrance of the Serapeum; and the boys who carried the lunch-basket, taking a short cut, had arrived there before us, and were begging to inherit the remains of the feast now to commence.

The conductor hangs up a Scotch plaid ulster on the nose of a granite mummy-case standing upright against the side wall, whose eyes seem to glare at the impertinence from their stony slits. Every one uses the antiquarian's deserted house quite freely, and the place is rapidly falling to pieces.

The Arab boys, denied legitimate admittance, peered into the house through the half-open doorway; and the stoutest-hearted among us were not proof against the hungry faces, and responded by dividing up the rations, — which were not too abundant or satisfactory, — blissfully unmindful of the results until we came out again to mount. There on the sand were the choicest meats thrown down among the half a hundred donkey-hoofs, in scorn of the succulent swineflesh considered unclean by the Mohammedans. When one goes to Sakkara with Cook, one does not sentimentalize, and the erudition imbibed on these excursions is small; for what the conductor possesses is appropriated by those of the excursion who have fought hardest for its possession, and followed most closely on the heels of knowledge as the conductor hastens through the sights.

It was' only after my return to the quiet Cairo apartment that a real appreciation of the Serapeum took place; and for that I owe thanks to the more scientific travellers who were there before me. The Serapeum discovered by Mariette Bey occupies only a small part of the Necropolis Sakkara; yet this corner is crowded with associations and symbols. Hewn in the rock are immense galleries, opening out from time to time into vaults, where enormous sarcophagi in porphyry are placed, which once held the remains of the Apis bulls, who had spent their twenty-five summers in the Memphis temples. On the sand above, a separate chapel was erected to each of the sacred animals, whose ashes were solemnly deposited in one of the lower cabins, dark as a ship's hold, to which a sloping passage descends as from a deck. Sixty-four vaults are only partly excavated, and hardly navigable by the taper head-lights, with which, in the rashness of enthusiasm, we were running in and out of the rubbishy places, in an unwholesome air and with every prospect of getting lost.

Near the side of the Serapeum, the despotic builders of the Fifth Dynasty were wholly in their element in constructing imperial tombs, and that of Ti in particular. This great personage has made his mortuary chapel to be surrounded by charming hieroglyphic pictures representing all the scenes of his life. We were hurried rapidly past skilful representations of human figures, drawn with great fidelity to nature, and presided over by the commanding figure of Ti himself, the proprietor of the tomb, who is represented, as usual, several feet taller than is consistent with truthful proportions to the Lilliputian stature of his wife and kindred. You see this lower feminine order in every case pictured as in real life, literally looking up to the demi-god. It seemed to me sometimes, as we scrutinized the tomb with a kodak, as if the spirit Ti himself, amiably disposed as he has usually been towards desecrating strangers, might decide even at this late day to flourish his baton of office, and avenge the intrusion.

And since the graves of the gods are not respected, who can hope to rest unmolested in Egypt? Twenty scenes of the Ti drama are carved on the walls; and one wonders what was the effect on the good Egyptian's mind in placing him in life on such familiar terms with his virtues and duties, and if he lived up to the high art of the decorations.

Near the entrance door is a farm-yard scene, showing the ancient Egyptians were initiated into the mysteries of fattening geese; and genuine *pâtés de foie gras* may easily have taken high rank among the flesh-pots which the Israelitish children were so loath to leave in their adopted country.

Spring-tide and harvest, reaping, storing, and transporting the Egyptian corn, sifting the grain and separating the straw by three-pronged forks, are represented faithfully on the smooth butter-colored walls.

There are no events in the old Egyptian life which do not enter into the area of the chapel pictures. The workmen of those days even credited the dumb creation with intelligent speech. The reapers say to the ears, "Now ye are large," or, "This is reaping; when a man does his work, he becomes gentle, and so am I." A driver of a herd of donkeys declares to them, "People love those who go quickly, but strike the lazy; if thou couldst but see thine own conduct!" This efficient plan of smiting the ass was followed by Balaam, according to time-honored custom, and since that time has rarely failed to produce the proper result.

High up on the northern side of the chamber are rustic scenes representing familiar occurrences, and filled with domestic sentiment. Softer and of a pale yellow color is a long procession of graceful figures of women accomplishing deeds of compassion, and offering sacrificial food from the family estate of the grand chamberlain, Ti; these products of the field will mysteriously refresh the dead one on his return, and to this good end are applied appropriate gifts. Brugsch Bey writes: —

"If we inquire into the motives of these inhabitants of the Nile valley in decorating the walls of their tombs with these curious scenes, it would appear that they intended to hand down to posterity a record of the earliest achievements of mankind in the promise of art civilization. Having hardly emerged from the simplicity of the primeval condition, they seem to have been proud of displaying the results of their peaceful conquests over the animate and inanimate world around them, and to have been desirous of informing posterity of these triumphs. At that epoch to behold was to admire. The chief occupation of the period was to embellish the tombs in the best possible manner, and it is these decorations which constitute the pictorial history of primitive Egypt; the instinct of perpetuating a name and family there originated the stone picture-books of Sakkara. Every Egyptian contributed in a more or less elaborate way to the records of ancient history, and the richer he became, the handsomer and more perfect was the structure which was to be the open sesame to their secrets."

But it is a long story, the history of mausoleums; the arrangements vary, the interiors differ, and the symbols are endless. Such a narration would include many interesting allusions to the deceased, his lengthy titles, and the honors of his grandchildren and near relations, numbers of prayers addressed to Anubis, the guide of souls in the infernal regions and the tutelary guide of the realms of the dead.

The most fertile mind could not imagine any exploits, incidents, or occurrences connected with the earth-life of Ti not included in the faithful drama, giving him an excellent opportunity to criticise his own biography depicted in the bas-reliefs.

The drawings in Baedeker supply you a working model of them, for the bas-reliefs are clear and brilliant only where skied; those on the line are badly smoked by countless tapers with which the Philistine tourists wander in and out of the storied rooms; studying their guide-book pictures, and leaving the originals blackened and stained by their carelessness.

What an instructive gallery it is! what a plunge

into secrets! what romance! what situations! It is a real resurrection of the dead, this mortuary chapel of Ti, and you have only to shut out the present in order to live in the past; to hear the words of all these personages who are so actually and faithfully fulfilling their tasks, unembarrassed by such a crowd of curious tourists.

These scenes penetrate what has been called the secrets of souls. But it is a long story, and many things I have forgotten; not one day, but years are necessary to know the open volume of the life of the mastabas, and long works exist, as guides through the deserted necropolis, which facilitate the mastery of the names and characters in the pantomime-drama. I will spare you a quotation of this momentous description, and refer you to the favorite Brugsch for the pleasures of erudite learning.

The yellow graduated limestone mass near the Serapeum and Ti Mastaba, which looks like a pyramid in disguise, is called the Step Pyramid, from the designers having shaped a new task to themselves, graduating the monument in a series of stages; but the novelty is not great. Any other pyramid when deprived of its external covering would look exactly the same; the peculiar facts about it are that it does not stand like all the others, exactly facing the principal points of the compass, and that its shape is oblong instead of square, giving it a sad and solitary appearance, as it stands utterly alone, and is the oldest monument in the world. No inscriptions furnish a clew to its uses, or why it was erected. No information can be drawn from the unique and complicated chambers of this companion of Gizeh that divulges its purpose. Two of the chambers are said to have been decorated in a gorgeous manner with green *faïence*, and inlaid in mosaic pattern. Relic-hunters have carried away pieces of it, and a richly gilded skull, and the golden soles of primordial monarchs stolen by the Germans, were unfortunately lost at the mouth of the Elbe, and only some chipped green-glazed doors and posts of rough limestone ever reached Berlin and the museum.

Many generations have been benefited and enriched by the treasures of Sakkara. Nearly the whole of the necropolis was explored by Byzantine Khalifs as well as by the modern explorers; yet it is a Cairo tourist firm that has given its name to the latest excavation, and Cook & Son's pyramid is the conductor's *pièce de résistance*, — the work having been undertaken, we are told, at their sole expense. It required colossal efforts to plod through the last sandy "sight," and listen to the conductor's weary recital of pure antiquarian facts, repeated in a monotonous-voiced monologue that suggested the remark of the poet about the katydid, "You say an undisputed thing in such a solemn way."

But we were soon scampering back to "Queen Hatasu" through the delicious clover fields. The sun smiled; the real live children of the villages laughed and shouted at us; and the oppressive old world was just fading out of mind, when a grewsome object belonging to the rider just in front flopped up and down with the donkey's gallop, before my dispirited eyes: it was a mummy hand appearing out of the rector's pocket.

A SCRIBE AND A COPTIC'S CORRESPONDENT.

A DAY WITH THE COPTS.

"WHERE are we going to-day?" I asked Miss T., whose saïs had driven her from the American Mission. "We are going to see the wife of a Coptic Bey who came to my school when a little girl," she answered, as I mounted the box-seat of the English dog-cart and gathered up the reins, which were intended to direct a little pony that knew the route better than I did, and that turned out cleverly for camel processions and hawkers of tropical birds, and a native cart, whose elongated shafts came in view around a sharp corner some time after the donkey harnessed to it had accomplished the feat himself.

Turning down the Boulevard Clot Bey, we passed plenty of obstacles in safety, reining in at each crossing, where a line of dromedaries, sometimes as many as twelve or fourteen, lean and wretched beasts, blocked the way. Upon the curious concave saddles, having on each side a looped thong for the accommodation of the Arab's thickest toe, which served as a stirrup, perched as many brown and blue Bedouins; no one can grudge the East the possession of their riding equipments. The two dangers in Egypt are said to be falling off a donkey and meeting a camel procession; and to avoid the latter it was no hardship to stop short at the corners, lie back in the little dog-cart, and let the loose-limbed complications glide by. As I looked around, varying specimens of the entire wardrobes of Eastern humanity shuffled by in slippers, for, in every Eastern city, money-changers, sleek and shaven of countenance, and cased in superior clothing, face this crowd of shoppers from behind very prominent glass cages. They are quite at liberty to cheat and defraud their unsuspecting Christian brethren, but the wise ones never return to repeat the first transaction.

A professional letter-writer, in the brightest of yellow slippers and whitest of cotton turbans, is making a love-letter for the young Coptic girl, sitting closely by his side, that her secrets may not reach those, who, unlike the envied scribe, have no right to them.

But the scenes are endless; spinning men and knitting men buzz past, plying their trade industriously to lose no time. Cigarettes are peddled as matches are in other countries, for the Turk's love for them is so strong that everything else except the nargileh gives way to them. A boy screams, "Gizian Gazette," — the Egyptian daily which controls the news of Cairo; not an American cable in it. Sufficient unto Cairo is the news thereof, but not so to travellers who have been at sea for ten days.

At each street corner is a pack of donkeys, ranged in a line, saddled and bridled as if ready to start in a race. If this species of ass-flesh could be obtained

AT A STREET CORNER.

in America, walking would become one of the lost arts. All these enumerated things passed by me, and doubtless many others, had there been time, would have crowded the picture and made it more piquant, more typical, and seasoned with the country.

Sixty seconds ticked away, while the camels stamped by at the street crossing, and I was again in the engrossing occupation of threading the long arches of acacia-trees, mindful of sleepy Orientals on foot or planted cross-legged at the corners, reining in to avoid running them down, — a performance they would have submitted to with great patience. "Mâ-shallah" — "God's will be done" — can also be translated fatalism, when the lazy Islamite retires behind his favorite expression rather than move an inch from the horse's hoofs.

The Coptic quarter is well shaded, the houses separated by gardens idyllically planted with honey-suckles and pink almond-trees, giving a pretty setting to the French balconies which rise out of them. A yellow dust powdered our hands and faces, and lavishly coated the Coptic women in white izars who passed this way; a speculative building mania has reached the old quarter, and the widest streets are blocked with stucco and mortar, — hence the dust, the infectious dust, of Cairo.

Many of the houses look as if they had been hastily abandoned at two stories and roofed over, so flat and uniform is the effect.

We stopped, or rather the pony did, at one of the more modern dwellings, in which impartial traces of Italian, Gothic, French, and Arabic architecture could be traced. The knocker was, however, brass, and unmistakably made in Oxford Street. A single rap brought a young Egyptian boy to the door, who showed us up three stone steps, and opened a heavy door provided with a lock and key of tremendous proportions. Inside, two women were curled up on the couches, listlessly fanning away flies. You would have thought I was an old acquaintance from the bright, warm greetings and the friendly, confidential manner with which the women extended their hands, touching one palm to the mouth and then gracefully to the forehead, saying softly, " Nehârak saïd," "Thy day be happy," between smiling lips and beautiful teeth. I was sure it was because I had the best of introductions, but Miss T. said, "No; every one is received in this smiling way." Any shyness or embarrassment which one might have imagined was left out of the situation; and I have never seen more charming manners among the corresponding people of Europe. The women are unconsciously queenly and dignified, — a pathetic contrast to the painful disregard for comfort in their surroundings. Taking advantage of a pause in the civilities, one glance about the room revealed to us its sins of omission in the matter of luxury, which were too many to relate. The place gave no indication of its external respectability. There were several long couches, all unpainted, a walnut chest, and on the far side, a frayed magenta rug, on which two children played, covered the straw matting, strewed with dusty litter. Drawn blinds shaded and concealed a little of the bareness; and here, in eternal eventlessness, lived the wife and sister of the most brilliant orator in Cairo, idling away their hours, and dreaming their day dreams in an automaton community where it is a heresy to differ from one's neighbors.

The girl mother had scarcely emerged from childhood, the long braids of tawny hair still falling under the gauze handkerchief folded Madonna-like across her forehead. The other was a woman, then five years widowed, with high-bred and clear-cut features, and a grace which made the contrast between clothes and body simply ludicrous, — a masquerade of shabby finery on a statue of Canova. Yearning for sympathy, cheer, and excitement with the pure hunger of a woman's nature, yet she rarely went out even into the small world of her own people. But in a life where so much patience is exacted, a little more in one or the other direction is not difficult. It was apparent they both knew English, but were always too bashful to speak it; and the Copts and I merely exchanged smiling looks, while Miss T. talked or read to them from the Arabian Gospels. I could not refrain from looking at their faces, their beautiful calm eyes and perfectly oval contours, which expressed such untouched child-natures; and one could readily understand that merely living in a sleep, and being left to themselves during the long colorless days, must crush out any effort to vigor or work. To become somebody under the sacred persecutions to which the Copts have so long been subjected, one must have a "heart of brass and a head of adamant." As Charles Wagner says on a different subject, "Where can ability, originality, and the desire to strike out find a place in a world so constituted?"

We are told the Copts derive their name from an old city in Upper Egypt, — Coptus, — their refuge from the flesh-pots of Alexandria. The early Egyptian Christians, escaping from the glittering wickedness of the capital, fled away into the Libyan desert caves, and there starved themselves into immortality. A few dreamy, inactive anchorites, like Saint Anthony, lived in solitude; but the real heroes banded themselves together, and had the courage to work, teach, and, to speak biblically, were "true yokefellows," like the saints at Philippi.

The contagion of this monastic life infected principally men, however; but a few women imitated their Buddhist sisters, and took vows which descended to them from India ready-made. When the Christian Church was broken up into colonizing sects, and the young contemporaries of Saint Clement adopted and established separate systems, the poor little church became weaker and weaker. The Mohammedans bided their time hopefully and cheerfully, and then burst on the fourteenth-century Christians, while the sword won more converts from its ranks than the pen had added to it in all the past years. The Copts alone, at least a great number of them, remained faithful to the faith once delivered to the saints at Alexandria. But the Copts were enthusiasts, — how else could they have kept their old liturgy and their ancient usages, which have been preserved since the beginning without material differences, as the Ethiopic rites seem to prove? It has been said the Ethiopians received their ritual with their Christianity from the Egyptians in the far-off past of A. D. 330, and have ever since been subject to the Alexandrian bishop. How long could this perennially abused people have lived without this tenacious enthusiasm, subject as they were to the tyranny of brown and yellow Arab masters, who permitted them neither to ride a horse nor an ass, nor enter a public bath without announcing their hated presence by a bell worn around the neck. It is even related of them that a law existed compelling Copts to wear blue turbans, as members of the despised religion, and while taxed and imposed upon with burdens of a financial kind, they also carried about the neck a wooden cross weighing more than five pounds. Indeed, nothing could have been stricter and more unreasoning than their disabilities in the way of education; until fifty years ago, not one of the sect was allowed to learn to read or write, consequently only a few aspiring priests know these branches, and the Mass service in Coptic is learned by heart. However, the younger generation of men love learning, and now that it is at last accessible to them, have entered government schools and even carried off the prizes, while nearly every accountant in Cairo is a Copt.

Although the Copts may be said to be the first Protestants, nothing could be more conservative than their theological behavior ever since; for since the schism of A. D. 457, between Constantinople and Alexandria, this earliest Christian church has neither begged nor borrowed doctrine or dogma from other creeds.

The translator of the "Rites of the Coptic Church," published in London in 1888, writes, "The similarities and even verbal identities of many phrases and petitions show that the Christian ceremonies were conducted throughout the East in the fifth century in much the same manner as at present; and more than this, the Roman ritual contains so many ideas, practices, and phrases identical with those of the East, it is clear that, in spite of verbal differences, and of various additions and omissions, the ancient rituals of all the unreformed churches are monuments of Christian belief and practice, handed down with unimportant modification from the sub-apostolic age."

Besides this internal evidence, many practices are proved by the allusions of early ecclesiastical writers to be of the highest antiquity. Such are the unction at baptism; the renunciation of Satan by the catechumen, who turns to the west and raises his right hand; the wearing of the white robe and crown by the neophyte; the bestowal of the ring at betrothal, and the coronation at marriage.

The Copts call a wedding a joy, and speak of marriage as such and such a person's joy; moreover, these amiable people express the truth of this idea in their contented family life: there are no separations, or very rarely; the tiny houses with simple rooms are the frames of happy, childlike natures, playing well their little parts, faithful over few things, and for that reason as great as any other children of earth.

The order of matrimony is composed of two parts, — the betrothal and the coronation, or marriage. From time to time, my curious mind has penetrated into the ancient liturgy, and accorded sympathetically with the strange old rites, which sometimes coincide and then differ distinctly from the religious services of modern times, and in the English translation that has lately appeared, the strikingly beautiful ceremony of marriage is set forth clearly and for the first time. It commences with a notice stating that, the gifts having been placed in the midst, with the golden cross and golden ring, the priest shall say the thanksgiving, proceeding to various betrothal prayers for the perfect consortship of the young people, especially that the wife shall be that good old English thing, — a helpmate unto the man; imploring blessings on the union, with many mercies, and, in the words of the prayer of consolation, petitioning finally the happiness of the bridegroom, who, the Prayer-book relates, has entered into the bargain "on account of the bitterness of man's life in loneliness." A marriage garland of silver gilt, ornamented in *repoussé*, is placed on the bride and bridegroom's young heads, and the priest then delivers the tag, or crown prayer, which is so tender and so touched with Eastern imagery that one cannot help quoting it for its own sake: —

"O God, the Holy One, who crowned Thy saints with unfading crowns, and hast joined heavenly things and earthly things in unity, now also, O our Master, bless these crowns which we have prepared for Thy servants; may they be to them a crown of glory and honor. Amen."

It is said the Copts of to-day, whose very name is an echo of the word "Egypt," trace back their lineage to the ancient Egyptians who built the pyramids. The ancient tongue is spoken at every Mass, and the singing, chanting, even the very folds of the vestments, have changed less than any other Christian church. How difficult it is to gather even a respectable handful of Coptic customs, even by raking the few learned pastures of Makriza, Wausleben, or Vanleb! They did their best faithfully to unravel all the facts that could be obtained of Church or State.

All that might have enlightened them and ourselves were in the manuscripts of the old monasteries near the Red Sea; and these purely theological libraries were burned four hundred years ago by the servants of the monks, in an uprising against their degenerate masters.

Since writing began, no book has been printed for the Coptic services. The manuscripts are written with a primitive reed pen, such as is used in the *ancien régime* of a dear, dead, and musty antiquity.

The Mass and Gospel are read in Coptic, but no one understands; the last person who is said to have spoken it was seen by Vanleb in 1763, but, being very deaf, he was not able to impart any useful information. In these days the vernacular Arabic is read after the Coptic. Clever and shrewd at his chosen occupation, fond of money in a harmless way, the chief reliance of Egypt in mathematical matters is a Copt. As merchants, they are original and enterprising, even to the matter of the bill, which is never sent in, but the man comes around to your house and says you owe him, saving stamps and long reckonings by his personal appeal.

The story of the Copts interests me more than mosques and citadels ever can. They are the inheritors of the faith, and the guardians of that first delivered to the Apostles, although it is impossible to understand how such an honor befell them. We were fortunate in knowing a well-informed Coptic official, who is one of the most progressive men to be met with anywhere, and I have noted his elaborate efforts to detail the difficulties between Church and State which seemed to be in the air, and, if not seen, can be felt by even an American. The good friend, being himself of the reform party, had no scruples about the powers that be, and, blending his account with that of the newspapers, has succeeded in disentangling the Coptic doings. It seems there is a great movement going on in Cairo to overthrow the heavy debts of ignorance patiently borne by the descendants of the faint pictures of fair saints, gilded on the missals of their church, — the faces of the type of Rameses and Pharaoh, which Butler says became the faces of anchorites, saints, and martyrs.

The Patriarch has been deposed; for a long time there has been discontent and grumblings in the flock concerning the one-man power wielded by his Excellency, Boulros Pashi Ghali, the Coptic Pope of this rich old church, which owns more than a thousand houses in Cairo. He alone has managed the financial affairs, and now inquisitorial societies have burrowed into the accounts; and the church, divided against itself on this question, has at last appointed a committee to look into its finances, of which the Patriarch haughtily refused to be made chairman; had not other Patriarchs managed with traditional inconsequence, their authority unquestioned, and their hands unopened except to crowd in the piastres?

We hear that this community, like the little Khedive, has drunk deep of the draught of independence, and so the Patriarch is banished to the desert, until at last he consents to become reconciled to the members of the liberal party, and to remove the ban of excommunication from Bishop Athanasius, who is its spirit. There only remains now the question of a general council in the community; or will the Patriarch insist on his unlimited absolutism, and keep the public funds and the administration of secular affairs in his own hands?

Yesterday his Excellency had a long interview

with Riaz Pasha, the Khedive's minister of war, as to the course to be adopted by him in future; but however it results, the condition of affairs can never be that which existed before the banishment. Straws show which way the wind blows, and a whole bale of mediæval straws have been swept away by this Coptic gust against clericalism.

There were effusive salutations at our parting with these ladies, for a visit from even a tourist is an excitement in their long daylight watches; and when we rose to leave, there seemed to be an interesting discussion going on with Miss T., which ended in our slipping again into the cushioned benches, and several cups of coffee determined the length of our stay. "The Effendi would be angry unless this civility was accepted," was the gist of their remarks; and when a little later, in complete ignorance, I ventured to hope the two ladies would come soon to see us, this unseen personality, the Effendi, was again evoked, and, as the custom is, the husband came the next day alone to return the visit.

Getting away at last from our friends and their refreshments, and driving slowly home, my mission friend interested me extremely in the advances made by the Americans in the direction of their religious affections: it seems that happily a remarkable change is appearing in the church; in some places they have called in a Protestant licentiate to preach after the Mass, and clamor for a Coptic Bible with a greed that the colporteur cannot satisfy.

To the general spiritual importance of this unheard of event is added another: thousands of the ignorant women are crowding the Mission Schools, particularly at Asyût, and, tearing themselves away from national ignorance and customs, aspire to be taught to read, perhaps even to write, — an acquirement hitherto in the keeping of scribes and priests, who have squandered all too short a time in attaining this rudimentary feat of learning.

IN A COPTIC CATHEDRAL.

AT seven o'clock a black tray preceded an Italian waiter through the double doors into my room, with three plates for two wafer pats of fresh butter, a crescent roll, and the tea steaming out of its pewter spout. Here was breakfast, the beginning of the day and an eye-opener to the indolent. Every morning the same sunbeams slant in between the half-open blinds, and the glow of summer beguiles away sleep; all the garden flowers send up fresh morning scents to the transparent blue of the summery atmosphere, which is Egypt. In truth, however, the best reason for this early beginning of days is a service at the Coptic Cathedral; and some moments later we brushed past the market stalls of the narrow streets just out of the Place Ezbekiyeh, paused before a rough arched entrance, stepping over dirty beggars crouching on the earth, and ran a gauntlet of crippled Copts in various degrees of wretchedness and disease, who whined for piastres with a practised tremolo of three purring tones. We have no conception of this outside the East, where the beggar is an established institution in the land, — the voluble exception to the silent Eastern people, an exception with whom the proverb is reversible, for speech is golden, and silence not even silver. A dair, or ring wall, encloses Coptic churches and monasteries; and behind it, in the centre of the open court, rises the ancient basilica, not big or ornate, or like any other cathedral, only gray and age-beaten, with black mosses between the arches of the stone platform which surrounds the building. In exploring several of the thirty-two Coptic churches in Cairo, we have found Abu Sergeh, or the church of Saint Mary, the model of all the later Egyptian-Byzantine buildings of the modern Copts. This basilica formed one of the resting-places of the Holy Family in Egypt, or rather the crypt is the supposed site; a damp and vaulted rock chapel, dark and dingy as possible, the opening so small that you must crawl in and stoop down, in order to discover the niche which tradition claims as the spot where the Virgin and Child reposed. The monk, appropriating the only candle, throws a slender ray of light on the diamond-powdered rock, and the frosty stalactites glow more brilliantly than the artificial frescos in the church above.

The nave of the cathedral is divided by wooden screens into three parts, — one a vestibule, or court, where a trough is usually placed for ablutions; the other set apart for the men; and the women are separated in the third from the body of the building by a grating, confined to a great black hole without windows, where, through the one entrance door, the silk shrouded figures file past, going in and out, all in black save the golden spool placed between the eyes above a crape scarf falling to the feet; so far can they go and no farther, and through the lattice openings, the incense steals in from the silver censers at the altar, and the gray smoke envelops the hopeless women huddled close together on the pavement, suggesting a human sacrificial rite, — a "suttee" of Egyptian Copts.

During the Mass, men and women promenade up and down outside on the board cloister pavement; there is often such a turmoil in the church that the priest steps down and implores the people to stop talking. In the church itself the congregation this morning were talking and moving about in seeming indifference, expending their devotion on leaving a suitable offering in the poor-box, though all the time in close proximity to the altar and within a few paces of the closed chancel, which was divided from the nave by a golden screen, where the frescos of fair-complexioned saints in familiar raiments smiled down on us in complaisant friendliness, the only near relations we had in that sea of bronze-colored brethren. A few tall Dutch stalls in the central nave were rented for a customary para, but the space about them was occupied by a red-fezed throng, standing so close that one can literally describe it as a red sea, at least that was the only comparison that rose to my mind.

Vainly we sought to maintain a good personal example of attentive devotion, but our knowledge of the service was elementary in the extreme; and as the Copts carry neither prayer-book nor missal, enlightenment on that score was impossible. The only thing for the audience to do is to listen to the Mass and Gospel as they come from the priest's lips in unintelligent Coptic, or look at the pictures or the ostrich eggs. From the Church of the Nativity at Bethlehem to the mosques of Cairo, there is evidently no check on the number of these curious ornaments of Eastern churches which usually hang suspended before the altar. In more than one church we were shown specimens, which sometimes were mounted on gilded frames, curiously carved samples of Moorish work; what is the influence of these original emblems on the religious bodies who approve them, is a problem, but a modern writer has found a fairly creditable solution, which contains besides a good deal of natural history in its engaging account. He says: "Instead of, as many think, the eggs proving a belief in immortality, I have read the Copts have a more natural belief. A priest of Abû-Sefên is quoted as explaining that the ostrich is remarkable for the ceaseless care with which she guards her eggs; and the people have a legend that if the mother bird once removes her eggs from the nest, the eggs become spoiled and worthless that instant; so the vigilance of the ostrich has passed into a proverb, and the egg is a type reminding the believer that his thoughts should be fixed irremovably on spiritual things." The use of the egg may well have arisen in Africa, where this fact has long been observed.

All this time the boy choristers, in black tunics and red hats, had formed two lines diverging from the opening of the screen down towards the congregation, who could witness nothing that was taking place in the choir, except the occasional apparition of the officiating priest passing before the hêkel.[1]

Understanding the power of backsheesh, an obliging Copt hurried us by a side entrance into the chancel back of the screen, where we were literally behind the scenes; in such a reward does one's experience with the silver para occasionally result. The sanctuary was dimly lighted, and covered with about sixty feet of Brussels carpet, framed in by a single row of seats covered with white muslin, and enclosed by a wall, doors, and curtains, the apse winding in steps towards a throne-place usually occupied in cathedrals by the bishop's chair, but in Eastern churches containing sacred images. In this place is the holy table, covered with a simple linen cloth, which is

[1] A sanctuary containing the high altar, literally signifying temple.

placed just opposite the screen door. Butler says, "Every altar in a Coptic church is detached, and stands clear in the middle of its chapel or sanctuary, and stands on a level with the floor." Although the side chapels are raised one step above the choir, the altar is never raised, but stands level. It is usually a four-sided arrangement of brick, solid and covered with plaster; on it rests the tabernacle, or altar-casket, with a rich cover in a jewelled pattern which men earlier far than the Copts have worshipped with sweet patience. The Patriarch's throne was placed with its back to the screen, and high dignitaries' chairs were dimly visible from where we stood, just beyond them, the only women present in that sacred place.

The priests were in motion most of the time, obscuring pictures, books, and saints with the thick smoke from the censer; you have not time to notice all the ceremonies, which succeed one another in rapid progression; but I can record faithfully my impression that the priest kissed his left hand at every solemn moment. I always waited to see it happen, and it never failed.

The Mass was celebrated by a priest in ample white brocaded cloak; the capuchin, which he pulled over his forehead, was glittering with cut stones, and ornaments of great size conveniently held this rather weighty garment from falling from the shoulder. I do not write precious stones, for the following reason:

The Patriarch's tag, or crown, takes the place of an Episcopal mitre. Long before I saw this one kingly symbol, which has outlasted every other mark of royalty, I had dreamed of what the brilliant shining thing would look like; and a feeling, half of irritation, half of satisfaction, surprised me at its appearance. The crown worn by the present Patriarch was presented by King John of Abyssinia, and looks its semi-barbaric origin. A silver-gilt dome is topped by a fine diamond cross. A combination of cylindrical bands further embellished the crown, set with a combination of stones of enormous size; and just in time to prevent a feminine burst of admiration, I discovered they were pure Palais-royal paste, and silence on the subject of the clerical jewels has brooded over my note-book ever since.

A dark-skinned and white-hooded man served as assistant; and the service seemed to consist in chanting, the removal of the embroidered cover from the ark, the responses being sung by the choir and congregation without instrumental accompaniment. Then the calm and white-bearded celebrant prayed murmuringly over the small round loaf of eucharistic bread, placed on a paten, with a Coptic cross to the Triune God on the isbodekon, or central part of the wafer.

The altar boys lighted candles, and followed him around the table, chanting until the bread was broken, and the wine poured out, when the korban was partaken of and distributed to a number of wee small children, girls and boys, whose bare heads were blessed while they circled around the table, each holding a small silken square before their lips, lest a crumb of sacred bread should fall to the ground. Meanwhile, the ranks of altar boys were increased by others, who came into the Holy of Holies, put on their white vestments in full view of the public, and walked about the enclosure with an unconcerned air. Just then the light came in strong, and a side door opened to admit the Patriarch, shrouded in a dark-hooded cloak, with shawl-like draperies framing the clear-cut and delicate features of a cheerful old face, whose bright eyes belied his long white beard. The crowd in the church who could not see him had felt his presence instinctively; and between rushing forward to the open screen to receive the bread, and striving to receive the patriarchal blessing, the tumult increased almost to a panic, while the distinguished prelate was protected only by two strong arms, reached out with an unconcealed intent to knock down the clamorous multitude in one strong blow. The service ended, the boys, who leaned their elbows on the altar, acting as human candlesticks, dropping the sperm on the holy books, whose writing they revealed to the reading priest, at last snuffed the tapers, and were again the little ragged street boys who would in another moment join their comrades in a game of marbles by the church steps. The men back of us were hunting in the dim light for their shoes, which had been removed during the ceremonies, and had disappeared utterly under the encircling line of benches; and we, not the detractors, but the faithful recounters, of this old-time liturgy, moved along with the throng, who had a better chance at his Holiness as he left the church, and with the rest of our brethren, stopped and kissed the Patriarch's hand, and received an old man's blessing, having understood at least as much as themselves of a service which is said in a language not only dead, but buried in oblivion, not even unearthed by the priests, who do not learn it, but have committed to memory the heritage which was given to the saints at Alexandria almost simultaneously with the day when the now almost forgotten precept was delivered, a precept which survives so literally in the eucharistic service of to-day, — the Master's command to "Suffer the little children."

In a morning of two years ago at this same old church, I listened to a voice that struck a note higher than the others, with more of feeling in the tone; I noticed it came from the little Coptic chorus-boy leaning against the golden chancel screen, who seemed to rise on tiptoe to pour forth his full strength in this chanted song of praise. A thin, pallid face it was, thrown back and lit up with such longing; his little frame vibrated with the inner emotion, and the quivering throat throbbed as does a bird that bursts forth in song.

Between the chants, his hands moved nervously and his features worked in painful excitement, so that it often happened that the moment to respond was slightly anticipated by the chorister. My heart followed the boy in his ecstasies: he seemed to reach what we could not see; and more real than the world about us was his world, peopled with the saints of Coptic teaching he had learned about in their glory of heaven. Rapt in the reality of the beatific vision, his sole joy was in the songs of adoring worship, which every day he sang to those he saw plainer than any in the great congregation, for he was blind. The boy had always haunted my memory; the year past I often dreamed of that spiritualized gaze and that ringing voice, and wished to hear it again. Now that I stood in the dear old place, I hardly dared to look up, for I thought the frail boy had gone to his boy loves, the maris;[1] but there he was, his pale brow carved like a della Robbia against a cloud of gold, still singing, the same pure look on his face, which was now pressed ardently against the pale cheek of the screen-angel.

[1] Mari, the Coptic word for saint.

JAFFA TO JERUSALEM.

LEAVING Alexandria, it is difficult to make up one's mind which is the most enchanting, to look back at the harbor, the Orientals, and the great pillar of Pompey behind the palm gardens, or outward on the endless blue of the Mediterranean Sea and the ship's bow ploughing its way through the waters.

March is the month for rains, and an atrocious shower soon obscured the charm of both views, while the exquisite skies of El Masr disappeared in the general oblivion. The steamers of the Khedivial line do not touch at Port Saïd going out, and we made the voyage in twenty-four hours, — a matter of felicitation indeed, when one is trusting a full complement of native officers and seamen in a queer, unsightly vessel, with a reckless-looking name in Arabic characters at the stern, and the Turkish crescent floating over rusty boilers and unwashed decks, from the mast where we missed the familiar colors which are supposed to indicate that "Britannia rules the waves."

The little vessel swayed and twisted in the heavy breakers, and nearly every one quailed before the miscellaneous contents of the *menu* presented at ten and five o'clock, in the dark *salon* bordered with narrow cabins, where the stoutest-hearted among us turned the color of "the pale horse of the Apocalypse" on entering. Early in the morning, we sighted the stretch of breaker-foam sea-coast, glistening in the spring sunshine of Palestine. The last hours were, as usual, the most trying, and the buffeting and knocking about experienced in the ladies' cabin made landing anywhere a thing to be desired.

Far in the distance appear the faint blue hills of Jaffa, — the bright sand-banks first, and then the Judean mountains. From the deck of our steamer, one can see the bright patch of town straggling up the rocky slope, and nestling among the orange groves, while the great ant-hill of Syrian deck passengers crowd towards the bow. However, it is impossible to define the movements of a Turkish steamer, — now full speed, now slowly, developing misunderstandings every moment more chronic between the engineer and the pilot.

An injudicious edict of Mohammed, prohibiting the use of bells, makes the signals an elaborate system of shouts. The Khedivial Line has not as yet adopted the device resorted to by the Head of Islam in Constantinople, who argues very plausibly that since electricity was not known in the Prophet's time, the Korân plainly does not include electric bells in the general prohibition. Finally we drop anchor a mile or two from shore.

There is no harbor here or elsewhere on this dangerous coast, and steam is always kept up, to avoid the chance of a sudden wind sweeping down and obliging the captain to run far out to sea, to avoid the fate which overtook the ancient mariner Jonah, whose story is one of the catastrophes incidental to this spot.

The proper quarantine officials make great difficulty about our landing at all, returning in kind the courtesy which other lands have so severely imposed on this supposed point of departure of Asiatic cholera. It is with real joy that we see two boats approach from the land, and a jostling, eager crowd of Turks in bright red jerseys, inscribed Cook & Son, appear on one side of the ship, while, on the other side, sailors labelled "Gaze" elbow their way to the deck; for the rival agents have to be placed on different sides of the vessel, lest they should devour one another. On these occasions, the excited Arabs rush about the decks, hoarse as wolves, shouting at each tourist, "Cook," "Gaze." Once divided, like sheep from the goats, in happy unconsciousness of what landing at Jaffa might mean, one by one the passengers creep down the ship's ladder, washed by breaking waves, and are seized by a couple of sailors and thrown unceremoniously into the arms of others stretched out from the great roomy boat the instant it is dashed up against the ship's sides.

A confused impression remains of the next experience. The steamer dips her ensign in farewell to us, and with slow, powerful strokes the crew give way; the slight Arabic form, almost a bas-relief, shows at each stroke intense strength, which seems exhaustless.

A wind has arisen, with rain, and the comparatively calm sea has become more perilous every moment. The red-coated sailors seem to climb up the crest of every towering wave, standing one at each oar, throwing their weight on every stroke and praising their Prophet in sharp, ringing tones, "Allah," "Allah." A reef of pointed rocks in part shelters the town; we dash through a slit of about twelve yards, and in a moment more are washed by the heavy surf right up to the stone custom-house steps.

There are few landings which present as many perils as this of Jaffa; and many stories of shipwrecks are told in the quiet, passive manner of the East, which make them only more thrilling, for, in the Jaffa way of thinking, our landing was comparatively quiet.

Jaffa is the genuine Orient; at least, the buildings by the sea have undergone no change. There is a frail, musty look about the old city, as if it had just been unrolled from its ancient winding-sheet, and, like a mummy, would crumble away and disappear if one only cantered over the rough pavements. No road leads into it, and the Europeans have exhausted their knowledge of diplomacy at Constantinople to obtain a concession for a harbor. Very flat, roof-screened houses, a few mosques, and some sad and forlornly clad natives make up the seaport of Jerusalem.

A mule may be hired at the water gate, but, owing to the slatternly pattern of the streets in this vicinity, a creaking hack can only reach you beyond in the suburbs. For your first pilgrimage, you climb the steep lanes leading upward to the plain occupied by the hotels, striving to keep in sight the luggage, each piece strapped to an Arab's back, there not being a single street where the slimmest and most diminutive baggage-wagon could roll and jolt along.

Everything is carried on the back; as some one remarked, "The camels are drays, the donkeys, carts, and the fellâhîn, trucks," in this primitive country of Haroun and Zobeïde. Fenced by high wooden boards towards the sea, are a few scattered houses of the type which are usually cramped and crowded into a factory village at home. A few yards inside the enclosure, we encounter one of these transplanted New England cottages, displaying the sacred blazon, "Jerusalem Hotel." Across the sandy roadway, the sun strikes a more familiar sign in clear and distinct letters, "Cook & Son." Nothing could afford a greater contrast, a more crowning absurdity, than these modern dwellings surrounded by tall palms and prickly-pear-trees, — an architectural anachronism made still more ridiculous by the absence of the usual hacks and horses of a new American village, which are here replaced by donkeys and donkey boys. A couple of urchins, with the merriest good-humor, gaze at our dusty shoes and grin invitingly; their meaning can easily be guessed at, especially as they carry a bootblack establishment, and offer a "shine" for a shilling, finally accepting twopence.

A little old lady, ensconced upon a settee outside the hotel, seems to belong to the surroundings, and an appeal to her to solve the apparition of the New England cottages brings out the information that they were transplanted bodily to Jaffa several years ago, by a Second Adventist Colony from Chicago.

Wood being scarce in Palestine, the only supply is from Russia; the Chicago colonists, following the shrewd promptings of local far-sightedness, brought with them the necessary household utensils, ploughs, furniture of astounding patterns, and flowery chintzes to suit the taste of the Adventist ladies. The "Second Sleepers," as they are dubbed by the natives, were soon scattered by fever and poverty: some returned to America; others have remained and gone to work. The plucky tourist agent, who defies the Palestine Protectorate of an English firm, is one; and another is the quaint little dame, clad in a faded gown and 1830 bonnet, who ekes out a pittance from the tourist, who usually buys her badly pressed Palestine blossoms after listening to a half-mumbled story which falls from the wrinkled lips of this self-exiled Niobe from Chicago.

The bedrooms of the Jerusalem Hotel are bare and plain as convent cells. A reminder of the former occupants (the Adventists) exists in the Scriptural names printed above the doors of each apartment. Dan and Ephraim are opposite to Judah and Ezra,—which would be edifying, if not so comical. All are alike in an original state of barrenness; the floor boards, roughly joined together, and a most unattractive-looking iron bed, fail to improve the general appearance. At lunch you are served with the usual programme of the season,—artichokes, stringy chickens, and eggs; and the landlord, as he hands the dishes, assumes a most unhappy expression if they are rejected.

After looking at Mohammedan Jaffa, the mosques and orange-groves, we discreetly amble along the steep path leading to the house of "Simon the Tanner," near the sea, with the hills in front and the Mediterranean beyond, pay a most moderate bill, and take the Jaffa and Jerusalem Railroad for the Holy City.

At the end of the nineteenth century, the prediction of Thackeray has been fulfilled: with a victimized shriek, a locomotive steams its steel anatomy along the iron road, tugging a train of six American cars over the first Palestine railway. The highway from Jaffa to Jerusalem was first a mere track, then a deplorable road was developed, and the first carriage appeared fifteen years ago. This lumbering and half mediæval equipage, which can still be seen at Jaffa, was often attached to a couple of gaunt horses, aided by a third whose only harness was a neck yoke and rope trace. The roomy landaus in present use have been in Palestine about three years, and until the railroad came, were an admirable substitute for their uncomfortable predecessors.

The railway was first planned through the plain of Esdraëlon, from Acre to Damascus, the Turkish government granting a concession to its Ottoman subjects in Syria, — a genuine Eastern bit of speculation, and one of the Sultan's pet hobbies, probably because the line was surveyed through his possessions in Palestine. The survey completed, the concession lapsed in consequence of difficulties, and therefore it has lost the distinction of being the first Palestine railway. The new railway is so opposed to Mohammedan ideas that even after the iron track was laid, a band of bigots upset the first train which attempted the journey.

It is not difficult to understand the astonishment of the Syrians at the rushing sound of the train speeding past their sleepy villages. At first it was something quite incomprehensible to them. Men sometimes slept in unconcerned security on the track; even now it sometimes happens that the engineer whistles and blows in vain, finally stopping the train, and calling out to a man on the track to take his neck off the rail. "Why don't you turn out for me?" he answers; "I can't trouble my sleep."

The concession for the Jaffa and Jerusalem Railway was granted by the Porte in 1888 to a company styled, "Société Anonyme Ottomane," having its headquarters at Paris. Although the firman was conceded to co-religionists, no Jewish syndicate in any part of Europe would have anything to do with it, from financial fears. From a religious point of view, Protestants raised an outcry against the enterprise, and refused help, while the great European powers declined to aid, on the ground of politics; so it is evident that the new enterprise would have suffered the same extinguishing fate as the former, had not the following remarkable event taken place. A party of extreme orthodox Catholics clubbed together, founded a bank with a capital of £800,000 and launched the railway by offering the shares to the English and French public; the publicans and sinners alike regaled themselves with the eighteen thousand debentures; and even the Holy Father himself is said to have been a large investor.

With the sum thus raised, the contractors agreed to build the road. The reasons which induced the Catholic Bank to undertake the scheme caused all sorts of rumors to spread about, and the European diplomatists looked with round, astonished eyes at the keyless enigma, finally deciding that the enterprise was undertaken to aid the ten thousand pilgrims in making their annual visit to Palestine. This solution met with great applause, and seemed appropriate to the religious Protectorate established over the Holy Land by the Latin Church.

The immediate country around Jaffa is flat, and planted with orange-trees in every direction, yielding the mammoth fruit which commands the highest price in Covent Garden Market.

At the shrine of Abu Nebût was dug the first spadeful of earth for the Jaffa and Jerusalem Railway, and the Graces showered on this portion of the country the fairest of fields and the reddest of lily blossoms, and the great arbiter of human health — the sun — is in evidence every day of the year.

There are five stations between Jaffa and Jerusalem; each one is a small structure, fenced about and well kept. The resources of flowers and foliage are made the best use of, and no unsightly heaps of rubbish litter the pretty grass round the little buildings.

Lydda, twelve miles from Jaffa, is the first stopping-place, all surrounded by pale olive-trees and the brighter foliage of palms.

The Plain of Sharon, through which we pass, shows more than anything else the contrast between luxuriant vegetation and absolute barrenness in Palestine. By far the most important station is Ramleh, but only faint glimpses can be had of the town and the crusaders' church, the scene of their two centuries of conflict with the Mohammedans; now it is the most go-ahead place in Palestine, although somewhat ruinous in appearance, containing a Greek population of about fifteen thousand persons, besides Moslems and Jews.

The train proceeds along with a calm and stately method of progression of about eight miles an hour. We are packed as tightly as we will fit, for the train is crowded, and we share our seat with the Turkish mail-bags, while the Tiberian mail-clerks, at odd moments, sort out the loose letters, and hand them over quite carelessly at the different stations. But we gain much by our leisurely railway travelling; it is delightful to follow the fellaheen at their odd ploughing and tilling, and catch long glimpses of the olive-trees, grown great and gray among the refreshingly green barley of the fields. Thirty-one miles from Jaffa, a headland of blue mountain flashes up from the valley, and blots out the view, but we keep right on, and one wonders how it is possible to continue through the rocks which entirely hide the little station called Dêr Abân, meaning, in Arabic, "the convent," according to our interpretation of the postman's broken English.

Fourteen miles from here is Bîttîr, scooped out, as it seems, from the surrounding Judean hills. The peaks and gorges make a wild picture, and the only sign of human dwellings are the Bedouin tents, — the same "black sepulchres" that the children of Israel probably possessed in this valley, for "Joshua blessed and sent them away, and they went into their tents."

For the last hour we have been winding and curving through the rugged hillsides. A convent cross on a dreary height, and yonder a garden slope, have foretold the city. Feeling there was a presence near, half fearing to look, no one has spoken, until suddenly the postman draws in his head from the open window and says quickly, "Look! how nice! from here is Jerusalem!"

The railway company have recognized the propriety of having their station outside the town, and every day at this hour a crowd of astonished

RAILROAD STATION AT JERUSALEM.

natives, bringing children and family, congregate to await the arrival of the slow, dragging train. It is as different as possible from one's preconceived ideas, this arrival at Jerusalem. Across the platform, the scene is made madly gay by an encampment of canvas-curtained wagons, whose turbaned drivers lean over the station fence and shout out the accustomed, "This way for the Jerusalem Hotel," "Going to Howard's." Once inside, the driver flourishes a whip with a defiant whoop, and the panting horses rush down the valley of Hinnom, and in ten minutes more the dreary tower of David looms through the cloud splendors of sunset; the great confusion of tongues at the Jaffa Gate, from the Jewish lotus-eaters, reaches our ears, and we draw up at Howard's Hotel on Mount Zion, just outside the town. The wall which actually defines the modern Jerusalem is that restored by the crusaders, and repaired later by the Mohammedans, making the city an irregular square. Every one knows this wall is pierced by one modern gate, and five ancient ones. The Damascus is the chief entrance for pomp and ceremony, but through the Jaffa Gate pours a constant procession of Eastern races, — money-changers, and women veiled with flowered gauze more or less soiled; and a piteous detachment of lepers are drawn up in single file behind their substantial tin alms-pails, expecting backsheesh from the crowd of shoppers sweeping around the market stalls, which form a sort of promontory dividing the stream of street loungers from the purchasers of imposing cauliflowers and musty onions, which are exhaling their share of the inconceivable odors represented at the market-place.

Near the Russian settlement is a fine entrance called the New Gate, and, half jesting, I ask the voluble guide, who has a legend for every other, if this one had any traditions; he would not commit himself, but replied, "Not yet, not old yet, but they are coming."

Opposite the old gate leading out on the Damascus road are the brown, low tents of a band of gypsies, in profile like angular mushrooms, spread over the slightly rising ground under the great wall's shadow. The gypsies are squatting on the ground in their usual languid groups, the gray heads and children in council assembled, and half submerged in smoke; their umber-colored cloaks tone with the dull shading of wall, earth, and tents, and the gypsies seem to grow out of the surroundings as a sombre type of earth's children, midway between the half-human faun and the European. The development of costume flashes out of the old-time gateway of Saladin. A group of native women are the vanguard of civilized dress in Jerusalem, having inclined favorably towards as pretty a rose and blue satin umbrella as one can see on the Riviera, while draped from head to foot in a white sheet which, according to the custom of the country, some day will be their shroud. The parasol forms a hopeful leaning towards European dress, and forestalls a not far distant day of independence for these Asiatics who have adopted so great an innovation over the ideals of a simple, worn-out past.

THE NEW JERUSALEM.

JERUSALEM outside the walls, as seen from the ramparts near the Damascus Gate, presents a curious contrast between the old and the new. The suburbs extend over an area larger than the city itself, spreading a mile in each direction, in unbroken stretches of rosy roofed houses encamped about the plains and creeping up the distant hill-slopes, like some new conqueror of the oft-conquered country. Thirty years ago there did not exist a single house outside the walls; the city itself and the vicinity were desolate and forlorn. Now a solid flank of hospitals, convents, and dwellings reaches out almost as far as the eye can see, everything smells of varnish, or is newly polished; and blows from hammers and chisels, marking even time with the Korân, sound from a hundred native workmen singing at their stone-cutting, while a pale, bearded monk, under a white umbrella, cuts the sky-line in his airy tour of inspection of the future monastery, reared to such colossal heights by his Moslem laborers.

These substantial dwellings, of immense square blocks of limestone, faint pink and brown in color, like variegated marble, speak in a fragmentary lapidaric way of the New City. Beyond are the sweet blue hills of Moab; the crest of Mizpeh, and the silvery shades of the Olive Mountains, sliding down to the Kidron Valley, are all shaded and soft with the wonderful glow of sunset, enveloping at last the old city of ruins itself, and blending the past and the present. I don't know what picture of modern Jerusalem other people have made in their minds, but to me it was a great surprise to find an electric light just outside the Damascus Gate, a telegraph line guiding the eye toward Mount Zion, and a railway whistle sounding over the Hill of Evil Counsel. These improvements owe their existence to Europeans; however, innovations, though quite unnecessary from the Turkish point of view, are not often opposed, — the Turks sitting quite still, like well-ordered school-boys, until their names are called, then, when they are told to do so, they come forward unhesitatingly, and applaud and sanction without stint. The Europeans are quite useful in doing the hard work, and the natives reap the golden returns with lazy appreciation of their benefits.

In 1869, there were not a dozen carriages in the country; now there is a cab-stand outside the Jaffa Gate, and the hotel where we are stopping is Western in every detail. On the first floor the usual Continental *table d'hôte* is served, with the ever-present *épergnes* of fruit, and sponge-cake pyramids, and the system of fragmentary allotments of fish and fowl prevails as in an Italian inn.

The triumph of having secured a dirt road between the seaport and the Holy City is now eclipsed by the construction of an iron one; the carriage road between Jaffa and Jerusalem was constructed at the time of a prince's visit to the Holy Land, — the farmers and fellaheen alike being forced to leave their own fields and prepare "to make low the hill, the crooked straight, and the rough places plain" for the honorable visitor. It was all done in true Eastern fashion, but done very successfully, and at a considerable outlay of capital which did not come from Turkish pockets. A story is told which illustrates the gracious way the Turks accept the improvements of civilization. A band of enterprising Germans, who founded a colony only a mile from the city gates, desired very naturally to have a good roadway to replace the donkey-track winding out to their settlement. They could not very well afford such an expensive luxury; and as the road would pass near by the dwelling of a very rich Effendi, and he would gain as much benefit as themselves, they summoned courage to ask his assistance. This request met with a prompt refusal; the natives did not require a road, and if the Germans wanted one, why, they must pay for it, and they did;

A STREET IN JERUSALEM.

but the Effendi does not disdain to use it every day, although he has not contributed a piastre.

Sentiment aside, Jerusalem impresses the majority of travellers as a dull, uninhabitable town. The Western mind frankly admits, when unassisted by spiritual cultivation, that the place might be made more inspiring if the postal service was reliable, and the newspapers unmolested. Turkish Jerusalem possesses the unique anomaly of two mail services existing side by side. Some enterprising Austrians have started a post-office, and it is considered a great advantage to send mail by their route. A letter addressed to England, and another to a station seventy miles distant, and sent by Turkish transport, were known to reach their destination the same day.

The telegraph was introduced in 1865 from Constantinople; but the electric wire is slower than the post, and one rarely trusts to it. In a secluded office, a native operator receives the messages which may be sent out to-day, to-morrow, or the next day, according to the activity of the one messenger boy employed by the company to deliver messages. One of the greatest deprivations to the foreign residents is the inability to receive newspapers. The Turks are exceedingly sharp in this matter, allowing only one to be taken at the hotel, which is published in Alexandria, and have effectively suppressed the attempt to print an English daily paper. Another, in German, was started, and stood the test for a time, but afterwards suffered the same extinguishing fate. On the other hand, considering the parcels post is cheaper to Jerusalem than to Gibraltar, though double the distance, it would seem that the residents of Palestine could safely indulge in blissful anticipatory indications of an amelioration of the above-mentioned failures.

Who would ever suppose that the suburbs of Jerusalem, which the Europeans occupy so securely, were only a few years ago the haunt of wild beasts, and that leopards and jackals prowled around the "waste places," while travellers were few and far between, and Cook & Son as yet unknown?

The true repairers of the "waste places" financially are the tourists and pilgrims, who leave annually $75,000 from their visits, besides the large amounts annually sent to priests, Jews, and religious and charitable institutions in Palestine. Isaiah was right: " for brass they bring gold " (stamped with the Victorian monogram), and for stones, the " iron " road has borne out the prophecy. An estimate of these golden bringers of prosperity to Jerusalem includes, besides Russians, four thousand Greeks, a few hundred Armenians and Copts, and nearly four hundred Americans, of whom two hundred and seventy were naturalized in the district during the past ten years.

Of the amount of grapes brought into the city last year, the convents took 500,000, public houses 400,000, and private families 200,000 pounds; all this shows the need of this increasing community, and gives encouragement to pioneers of progress in the Holy Land.

Certain straws show which way the wind blows; and the permanence of these signs of land investments shows them to be more than straws. When we consider that Jerusalem has almost no manufactories, little foreign commerce, and a population of poor people, the price of land is astonishing. Speculation, deathless even in this Oriental country, is everywhere to be met with; properties change hands every year, and the prices demanded and obtained are exorbitant. For land within a quarter of a mile of the city in any direction, according to the Consular Report, the following prices are quoted for 1893: two acres sold in 1890 for $250 an acre, in 1891 for $750; twelve acres sold in 1890 for $455, and in 1892 for $2,178 per acre. Several acres of this land sold in 1886 for $363, and advanced in less than ten years to $6,534 per acre, while land outside the Jaffa Gate, an excellent location, sold in 1865 for $1,000, and in 1891, $24,000 was received for it. Almost the first building erected outside the walls of Jerusalem was the school founded by Bishop Gobat, which still stands on a little corner of Mount Zion under the shadow of David's tomb; Talitha Cumi, the German hospital, is neighbored with lordly buildings, which have sprung up during the last twenty years in this retired spot, where now the rows of stone houses rise up before the pretty rose-planted gardens and hide the vista, while the busy settlement about the hospital gives life and movement enough and to spare. The great land barons of Jerusalem are the Russian monks, who, in intervals of mystic revery, have acquired almost one-fourth of the city. Some inner vision has revealed to them the speculative advantage of an addition to our hotel, which they already own; and a spiritual father may be seen any hour supervising the masons with a trained overseer's eye and a business faculty which seems to co-exist with a special devotion the Russians have toward the Holy Land.

For a quarter of a century this power has apparently rivalled the Latin Church in profitable investments. At the gates of the Holy City on the northern plateau, which has served for the encampment of the destroyers of her peace in every age, the Sublime Porte has ceded to Russia an immense tract, which is surrounded by a high wall enclosing a great cathedral, consulate hospitals, and convents, for the thousands of pilgrims who make it, at Easter time, a populous little Russian village condensed between the giant walls.

It is a disturbing problem to all sects alike, — the dangerous encroachment of this ever-militant church, which has built a great square tower on the summit of Olivet, in the most favorable spot for the observation of the whole country, — the Dead Sea, the mountains of Moab, — and has chosen other military perches for watch-towers in different parts of Palestine, and scarcely veils the real destiny of the immense sums raised at great sacrifice from the peasantry every year for works of piety in the Holy Land.

The time of Easter is approaching; and before day breaks, a procession of fantastic pilgrims, at once smiling and tragic, pour out of the Russian quarter, chanting along the way towards the Holy Sepulchre, the powerful tones of the men blending so harmoniously with the silvery voices of the women and children. They seem like an incarnation of Tolstoi's stories: here is Petrovanish, who donned his thick fur coat, wrapped the heavy cloths about his legs, and tied on the sandals the morning his pilgrimage began, when the whole village accompanied him a day's journey on the steppes. Only a few hours more, — when his pictures have been passed trembling into the Holy Sepulchre, the lights have sparkled on the Madonna's golden tiara, as it was pressed on the Holy Shrine, — and, with these blessed pictures carefully tied in a handkerchief, — one for each in the Russian village at home, — and a gigantic cauliflower under one arm, the peasant, with glowing face, returns again to his convent, full of gladness, to dine on the fresh green cabbage.

The Armenians occupy the garden place of the city. What are Russian gilding and fabulous jewels to the clumps of rich palm and date trees, clustering about the convent avenues and the flower-topped Italian walls? They, too, have acquired a great property; and pilgrims are housed in a building adjoining the convent, in family apartments shown us by a priest, who estimated five thousand yearly visitors for the Easter pilgrimage.

It is incredible how anything could be accomplished, in view of the Turkish opposition at first directed to all monastic acquirements of territory. The same hooded men who now reap the reward of perseverance were obliged to bring in each stone for the new convent by hand, throw it in some careless way about the grounds, in order not to excite suspicion of their plans, and only ventured to build after the materials were safely introduced inside their strong walls.

The material of these great religious houses is stone, nearly porous, so it would take several years for it to become proof against dampness, were it not for the old quarries, which furnish cement to glaze the outside walls and prevent their destruction.

SOME JEWISH COLONIES.

NOT very many years ago, the Jew was never mentioned among polite Eastern nations without some parenthetical excuse, "I have met a Jew (begging your pardon)," "This man is a Jew (begging your pardon)." Although this apologetic form of presenting the Hebrew dates back to an age beyond our own, there is still much to be desired in his treatment; and though the Hebrews are not actually pelted with stones, still, the diluted quality of the mercy vouchsafed to them is the most discouraging part of the process of burying the religious hatchet.

A few people have undertaken to prove that the Jews did not come into the world with saddles on their backs; and to-day the colonies in Palestine have made probable the near celebration of a banquet of reconciliation by the favors shown them by various colonization societies of England.

To go from within the walls of Jerusalem to its suburbs is to leap over two thousand years, notwithstanding the close proximity of the city to its modern offspring. For my part, the greatest surprise awaiting a first visit to Jerusalem is this very contrast and its supreme meaning. Coming from the narrow network of tunnelled alleys, enclosed with dingy walls, probably haunted by epidemics, the new city outside the Jaffa Gate, with its great clean hospices and prosperous-looking dwellings, seems a paradise of pleasure in exchange for the opposite of dreary ruins.

The first of the suburban buildings to attract attention resembles a barrack for soldiery on the slope of a hill behind the excavations for the tomb of Herod's wife Mariamne. These low one-story dwellings are the Montefiore almshouses, the first buildings erected outside the walls. Sir Moses Montefiore built them in 1865, as a refuge for poor Jews, to whom they are absolutely free, one family having lived there for nearly thirty years. So it happened, strangely enough, that the first charitable institution for the poor in Jerusalem was a hospital founded and supported by the great English philanthropist, and he was a Jew.

Near by, a Dutch wind-mill produces a queer effect: it serves the neighboring German Templar Colony, where the smoke curls cheerily from the little red chimney-tops, and the vines cling caressingly to the tiled beams; and one thinks life must be very sweet and cosey within the tastefully painted houses, so German in appearance you almost fancy you can hear the Rhine songs.

The interest excited over the return of the Jews to Palestine has been manifested in a hundred ways, and is looked upon with great favor by the European nations. Colonization societies have continued to be formed, and funds have been collected with such alacrity that as a consequence the Jews have arrived in Jerusalem in such numbers that there would have been a famine awaiting the returning Hebrews, had not the cry of Judea for the Jews reached the land of the Czar, — the fatherland of everything oppressive, — and there sprang up among diplomats the fear of finding Palestine already occupied when the time should come to wrest it from the mummy nation which now holds it by sufferance only. Under this influence, the Turkish government issued a firman prohibiting the erection of houses for the Jews, followed the next year by an order denying the right of Jews to buy land; they might sell, but every citizen in the Holy City should pledge themselves not to yield an acre to the Hebrew.

If cities are to be determined by the majority, Jerusalem is again a Jewish city. The firman enacted in 1891 to prevent the Jews from emigrating to the Holy Land is not acknowledged by the English as referring to other than Russians, but they all know how to percolate through the boundaries of Palestine, in spite of law and firman.

Among the Jews, there are many who interpret the

prophecy to restore their sacred country, which is foretold by ten out of the sixteen inspired seers, as being fulfilled in the present day, however doubters and scorners exist, for this nation has ever inclined towards the worship of false prophets — and pelted their own. "Oh, Jerusalem, thou that stonest the prophets!"

The Jewish people in and about Jerusalem number about 40,000, nearly one-half of the entire population. Ten years ago, there were perhaps not more than 1,200, — a number now doubled and trebled by the returning thousands to whom the country is a fatherland, including Lebanon down to the Jordan Valley, and bounded by the Arabian Desert and the Mediterranean Sea.

Five distinct classes of Jews are to be met with, who, with the exception of the Yemens, have their own rabbis, treasurers, and tribunals. The Sephardim are the most prominent in number, as they comprise the Mugrabîn and Karaites Jews, who reject the Talmud, contenting themselves with the Old Testament. These claim to be the original Israelites driven out of Spain in 1497 by Ferdinand and Isabella. The second division of the Hebrews is the Ashkenazim, which includes Germans, Russians, and Poles. The Polish Jews are again subdivided into three religious sects, — Perushim, Chasidim, and Khabatiaks, — which do not differ in the essentials of religion, but disagree about different ceremonials and the obligatory character of rites.

Besides the almshouses, the charity of Sir Moses Montefiore, several other bankers have built hospitals and numerous schools for girls and boys in the district towards the west, the garden of the country-side; here they teach Hebrew, Arabic, and French, besides a congenial trade, according to the different tastes of the scholars, which assists them in time to gain their own living. Only in the educational branch of philanthropy are the Jews slow and hesitating. The rabbis fear education, from a religious point of view, and the necessary finances are a serious problem to deal with; but still they are not slow to perceive the numerous advantages which the exertions of other churches reap from the privilege accorded to all comers of education without price. Bishop Gobat has founded a school on Mount Zion; houses of industry, with clean and properly fitted technical schools, are established by other Christian denominations; and finally the Jews, aroused from their lethargy, exert themselves to compete with other races and lessen the influence of Christianity in Palestine.

There are, in all, eighteen Jewish colonies now in Palestine, distributed in the different districts of Jaffa, Galilee, and Carmel; and two others are projected in Gilead, where settlement lands have been already purchased. The original establishment, where the first *bona-fide* attempt was made to engraft the art of agriculture on the Hebrew, received the optimistic title of Mikweh Israel, at Jaffa, where, notwithstanding Turkish opposition and a natural unfitness for the work, the founder established an agricultural school with over sixty pupils, and had dominion over two thousand dunems of land. (Turkish land of any value is sold by the pick, or dunem; four and one-half dunems make one acre.)

This land is laid out in vineyards and orchards, and, above all, these colonists are willing to renounce the haluka, which is sent to Palestine by the Jewish people in other lands, and distributed to the Hebrews during the month of Moharram, — the sum varying according to circumstances from one to four pounds, which does not fail to effect sloth and indolence, the great cause of much of the failure of the colonies in Palestine.

Among the colonies of the Jaffa district, that of Rishon le-Sion cultivates the black and white grapes on a large scale, producing an excellent claret, which has attracted attention in Egypt as well as Palestine. Even steam machinery is used for irrigating the land, and furnishes the water supply for domestic use, so the colonizing Hebrews are not behind in utilizing modern machinery in a way little dreamed of by the prophets who foretold their returning to "gladden the land."

Nahalath Reuben, half an hour distant from Rishon, has solved the question of associating Jews and native fellâhîn in field labor. Laurence Oliphant, who has seen them, says: "It would be difficult to imagine anything more utterly incongruous than the spectacle thus presented, — the stalwart fellâhîn, with their wild shaggy locks, black beards, the brass hilts of their pistols projecting from their waistbands, their tasselled kufeihahs drawn lightly over their heads, and the ringleted, effeminate-looking Jews, in caftans reaching almost to their ankles, as oily as their red or sandy locks, or the expression of their countenances." After wretched difficulties about the division of the labor and the proceeds, the leopard and the kid lie down together, and have respect for a covenant agreement as to the profits of the oranges and vegetables in which the sons of Judea are established in sevenfold possession.

Kastania and Gadara are the soft-sounding names of other colonies in this Jaffa district. In many cases the charitable machinery of Europe has been set in motion to aid settlers. The Hobbe ve Zion Association advances loans of money, to be repaid when the land becomes productive. In other cases, owners of the land employ Jewish labor for the field work, and send out stewards for the purpose of managing the colony; one estate is called the "Society for Menucha ve Nahalah (Rest and Possession)."

The land purchased has been carefully selected, and is eminently fitted for colonization purposes. A mere footpath leads into Latroun, an hour's ride across the country. For several years the colonists have been living here in sheds, seriously annoyed by roving Arabs, but are compensated by the perfumed air of orange and lemon groves, which would even make seductive the whitewashed stable of the poor manager if this primitive vicarage were only in the orange gardens of Jaffa.

Other colonies are the sole possession of Baron Rothschild, who, by a stroke of genius, has found the culture of the grapes so congenial to his poorer brethren that he employs Jewish laborers at one franc, fifty centimes per day, until they become in a short time self-supporting. Various experiments have been tried, such as flower-raising for perfumery, and fruits for market, but without good results. The land is unprofitable when asked to produce cereals. The grain garnered in Palestine is a mere flash in the pan compared to the harvest garnered with little effort in the rich Nile Valley; so grapes for wine, and mulberry-trees for silk worms, and, in some places, soft-shell almonds, are the abounding products of Palestine that pay to export to a foreign market. It does not seem difficult to shake up energy and agriculture in the dwellers of certain independent Jewish settlements. Thrift lies in the germ of their natures, and at the

Rothschild settlements the colonists are in such a prosperous condition that no Arabs are employed, neither do they receive any outside support; in fact, the Rothschild colonies are worked exclusively by Jewish labor, with the sole exception of skilled mechanics, who are given temporary work at carpentry. Families receive a monthly cash allowance, — somewhere about eight francs a month for each man, woman, or child of the original colonists; to the late comers, something less is conceded.

At the Baron's expense, rent free, the Jews occupy large dwellings built of stone, somewhat barrack-like, but comfortable, — a veritable paradise to the poor hunted Jew, arriving destitute and forsaken, who is provided, at the cost of little personal effort, with shelter and plenty of food.

With all these natural advantages for the returning Jews, it is not to be expected that an Israelite will place himself in a Christian colony, unless there is something to be gained by doing so.

Eighteen miles south of the Holy City, on good arable land, through which runs the Jaffa and Jerusalem Railroad, is Artûf, — an estate of some twelve hundred acres, managed and owned by the Jewish Refugees' Society of London. After enormous trouble and expense, this land was peaceably occupied by blocks of houses, not yet plastered or tenanted except by the scorpions in the walls, but nearly ready for a colony to materialize. The colonist, attracted by the new scheme of a twenty-one years' land purchase, having signed a contract for one of the houses and a small piece of land, finds the advantage of this system to consist in being able to possess his ancestral land after a term of years, having been supplied in the mean time by the Society with implements, animals to work, and substantial food.

"Yawash" — slowly — is a good motto for hasty decision regarding the future of Jewish emigration to the Holy Land. Palestine is quite unequal to the support of ten million Israelites, is the comment of the Europeans; nevertheless the Promised Land includes an acreage equal to England, Wales, Ireland, Belgium, and Holland, and these countries support 50,000,000 inhabitants.

The natural resources of the fair country which Sir Percivale in his Holy Quest calls the blessed land of Aromat, may be recorded faithfully as unbounded; every climate is represented, from the Alp land of Lebanon to the tropical Jordan Valley with its stores of beautiful fruits and creeping greenery. It is the country of countries for oranges. The few square miles planted around Jaffa bear the largest and best fruit in the world, and bring the highest prices. Never was there such a success as came to that little spot under cultivation, where the value of the oranges shipped to Egypt and Turkey alone amounted in 1881 to £60,000, and the amount sent abroad has doubled and trebled in the last years; some one has estimated that, taking the seaboard as one hundred and fifty miles long and only five miles wide, and supposing this piece of land to be planted with oranges only, the profit derived from this one article would amount to the astonishing sum of $9,000,000 per annum. Grapes also grow with the least possible care, and so luxuriant is the annual yield that farmers allow the luscious fruit to decay, because it would be of no pecuniary advantage to take it to market.

All the country is fertile, besides being well supplied with minerals, while the railroad makes its riches accessible to all the world; and one can trust the shrewd Jew to know how to take advantage both of his rare opportunities and the fact that his fatherland lies midway between the inexhaustible treasures of the East and the great wealth of the Western countries.

THE BOX COLONY.

ONE of our last days in Jerusalem I took advantage of the beautiful weather to make an expedition I long had contemplated. It was to see with my own eyes the little red-roofed colonies, spotted over the grassy ridges towards Gareb. The excursion was presided over by a Syrian, or rather a Samaritan, half of whose daylight hours are spent in the saddle of an astute young donkey, who treads in his own footsteps among the unfrequented villages of the refugees. It is growing warm, and the road northward through the Russian settlement is dry and dusty; the white convent walls shut out the scenery, and leave nothing to be said in favor of the slow mode of travelling on donkey-back, for the present Syrian beasts do not possess the desirable characteristics of Mohammed's ass, called El Burâk, "the lightning." "Sir Balaam" in Palestine is not only deaf to music, but also to blows. There are strong reasons for believing, however, that a secret understanding exists between the donkey and his little master, who is never caught in the act of being stupid, and a backsheesh always develops an unaccountable alacrity on both sides. Soon the view opens on a lovely fresh landscape, showing the great green undulating downs, sweet with clover and wild flowers. The first instalment of cottages on the road lying in the sunshine about us is called Meashrim, meaning an hundred doors; now it numbers a thousand. It was built by rich Polish Jews, and is situated about ten minutes' walk from the Jaffa Gate.

A low one-story stone building is occupied by the refugees on the instalment system, those who pay the full amount in time becoming the owners. There seems to be barrack room for half a regiment in this soldierly looking dwelling. Evidently comfort was the last thing thought of in this establishment, and that it is not a failure is due to the energy, perseverance, and pluck displayed by the colonists in face of provoking obstacles placed in their way by Turkish authority.

There does not appear to be the great joy and gladness on the countenances of this "returning remnant" spoken of by the prophets; still this little spot represents the only shelter and safety in the whole country to a hunted nation.

Farther on, Niveh Sedet, a cheerless little colony, is called ironically the "Pleasant Land of Beulah." I fear it is only a figure of speech, when the tropical summer sun shines on the treeless surroundings, and the hot air broods over everything, drying up the thirsty roots and leaves of the unshaded earth about them.

At the end of half an hour I can see from my saddle, perched on a hill-slope, the curious little houses of Shepet-Tsedek, nicknamed the "Box Colony." No road leads into it; the meadows are unseamed and unscarred by wagon wheels or the winding tracks of donkeys.

This glittering village is built of petroleum boxes, flattened out and nailed on a slight wooden frame; roof and side walls, chimneys and casements, are constructed entirely of glazed tin, and one can easily imagine the crackling which must result in a hailstorm. The wooden doors were provided by the London Jews' Society, to which my companion belongs, and to which these Yemen Jews owe everything. These Jews originally lived in Aleppo, where they were well off; and when asked why they emigrated, they answer, "We would rather suffer here than be prosperous in our own country; it is because we love Jerusalem."

The only street in the colony is filled in with various rough pointed stones; even a donkey has great difficulty in picking his way over them without a stumble as he wades into the liquid mud half concealing the various holes and ditches. At right angles to this street are narrow intersecting lanes, bordered with the bright tin box houses about ten feet high and a dozen in width, floored with mother earth and without windows; the side walls, lined next to the rusty tin with stones, are kept in place by occasional strips of lath.

In one of the gas-box houses, fifteen Jews are living, one and a half square yard to each person. The family of four generations came here, it is said, without the authority of the Pasha, and were peremptorily turned out. One of our donkeys looked in at the open door and effectually filled up the aperture of a house, where fifteen grown persons live their lives, like bees in a hive. Piled up at one end of this room, is a heap of stones covered with rough boards, making a sort of platform, which is the "upper chamber" of the house, and the most popular idea of a bed consists of a heap of rags with a skin to throw over one when it rains; while in a dark corner, hardly visible in the dark space left for it, a baby swings contentedly in a coarse hempen bag. In the remaining six feet of flooring, a woman stoops over a clay oven about a foot in height, containing a few charcoals, over which a saucepan rests on a strip of tin, simmering the coarse ground maize, mixed with a little wheat flour, which is the staple of life in the "Box Colony." I stood watching this rude and simple process for some time without disturbing the operation; but when my companion came up, the cooks left their fire, the mothers their babies, and the loafing ones their dreams. It was well worth coming down here just to see it; the sick ones crowded around for medicines, and the helpless ones for alms, with a touching devotion. A king would rarely obtain such real love from his subjects, although they might show it in a more civilized way, and wear gold lace and tinsel; while these are clad in clothes to which cast-off is the only word applicable, — a procedure about to be acted upon by the clothes themselves.

It is all so queer, such an example of strange upside-down fashion of colonizing, that justice cannot be done it in description. It gives one a terribly real idea of the chronic state of famishment in the little town, where no gardens or markets, or even shops, are to be seen. The men labor in "Abraham's Vineyard," I am told, work being provided for them by the C. M. S. Society of London; however, I fancy the colony is taken care of collectively as well as individually by the same Society.

Four piastres per day is the usual wage, amounting in some cases to ten piastres for skilled laborers, who work eight, nine, and sometimes ten hours a day in the summer-time. A wire stretched on tall poles, representing the city wall, completely surrounds the colony. It looks like some ghost of a telegraph service. Beyond this line, no son of Abraham is permitted by Jewish law even to carry a handkerchief in his pocket on the Sabbath Day, — a law which is elastic enough, however, to allow the article to be wrapped about the head. No Jew is allowed to open a letter, as that would break the paper; however, he may read it, if another person destroys the seal. Beyond this imaginary wall, the law forbids tying or untying a knot, or even carrying a stick. .

An ascetic rabbi with a "turtle-dove" beard, as the Orientals would call it, and two oily curls plastered over each ear, who unfortunately inclines to a wretched mixture of civilized and Eastern dress, attends to the observance of ceremonials, enactments, and dietary laws.

We found him seated on the only straw mat in the colony, in a little zinc synagogue ten or twelve feet square, which is attached to the earth as mysteriously as Mohammed's carpet, for no one knows what keeps it from blowing away in a gale of wind. The most primitive altar of unpainted boards, holding two bright tin match-boxes as alms basins, is placed in the eastern end of the building, facing the Temple at Jerusalem, as Solomon directed; and the only churchly vessels are a couple of silver spice-boxes attached to a framed Hebrew manuscript title to the building, placed above the Holy of Holies. Here and there are precious relics, to be looked at from a distance and admired with respectful gravity; while a feature of more than ordinary interest is the Passion Service, on the concluding portion of which the old English nursery tale of the "House that Jack Built" is founded.

Squatting on the floor of the synagogue, which is also a school, is the teacher, sewing clumsily on a white shirt, and at the same time urging on seven little Israelites from six to eight years of age, who are seated around a huge volume chanting Leviticus in Hebrew, wofully out of time and tune.

The Yemens have no books; the only copy of the Old Testament has been written by hand, and the boys have learned, from sitting one at each side of the manuscript, to read it equally well, no matter which way it is turned, — one upside down, another sideways, and the others in its normal position.

The old Rabbi was on his feet the moment he saw us, every wrinkle expressing joy, pressing our hands first to his lips, and then his forehead. The Jews have imbibed some of the Oriental expressions of hospitality; in very flowery metaphors, we were pressed to enter and partake of sticky little lumps of sugar, which clung to our fingers like myriads of burrs. The poor Jew seemed intelligent, and, like the Yemens, was open-faced and unassuming, and, besides, had a decidedly self-respecting appearance, quite above his poverty. In an adjoining house was the Rabbi's home, without a sign of homelikeness about it; his wife, a lovely Jewess, looked up from the *débris* of boxes and vegetable remains strewed over the dirt floor, and talked rapidly to the Rector, who afterwards told me that a child of the eldest son had died, and, according to Jewish law, the relatives must mourn seven days, during which time no work or even baking is allowed, and having nothing ahead, they must be helped or starve.

The maintenance of this colony has been a perpetual drain on the London Society, and the supporters of it deserve great credit. I hope it may occur to some one to help them in this work.

On the Bethelehem Road, three colonies have sprung up in fourteen years, and are growing gradually; another, the Damascus settlement, exists on all sorts of work. A few among the more industrious colonists have a little money, but they are never too well off to have a house given them.

At Mahadet-je-Judah, the Hebrews are provided for by subscriptions among their co-religionists in prosperous lands, having a substantial-looking settlement near the Jaffa Gate, where the splendid grapes grow so easily and luxuriantly. The Jews delight in fruit cultivation, which is much more congenial to their tastes than agriculture, and they manage so it is a pleasure as well as a profit to win piastres from the willing soil. A watch-tower (merely an enclosure of rough stones) stands now, as of old, in every vineyard; and when the grapes begin to ripen, the entire family go forth to occupy it, each taking his turn during the clear nights at the post of observation, for signs of thieving foxes, robbers, and perhaps the marauding specimens of their own race.

In and among the hills surrounding Jerusalem, there are nearly one thousand Jews coming there from the degenerate slums and filthy hovels of Europe; still in great poverty, if not absolute want, a strange and characteristic trait accompanying all alike. You rarely, if ever, meet one of the inhabitants of these colonies begging for backsheesh; and of the seven thousand mendicants in Jerusalem who molest one at the gates, amid the clamorous grunts for alms, I have never seen the corkscrew curls of any Jewish beggar.

Each hilly slope has its group of tiled houses, nestling on its old historic sides; most modern-looking sides they are now, and very civilized indeed is the English cottage at Goath, which comes in view as we canter up the neat roadway leading through lovely patches of meadows reddened with the scarlet anemone, — the lily of the field in the Song of Songs, — and we are well content to drop the reins on the donkey's neck, and gaze on the rich blue of distant Mizpeh. This is Goath, — the last colony we shall reach this morning, but not the least interesting. The estate belongs to the London Society for Persecuted Jews, and is superintended by two trained missionaries, who are good amateur archæologists in the bargain; three hundred fruit-trees and three thousand vines are cultivated by fifty-six Hebrews, who labor, besides, in making smooth the stony places in the neighborhood for future Jewish colonists. A part of this process consists in blasting away the rosy lime rocks which peep out from the hillside. At a little distance from us the match is applied to a fuse; a sudden flash, and the exploding gunpowder tears away the soft stone, disclosing a rare scorpion in the smoking centre, who was soon impaled upon a wine cork in a glass case.

Close behind the cottage, the dwelling, and also the superintendent's workshop, is found a precious discovery of Roman occupation, called, from the rich decorations of the mosaic pavements, "the King's wine-press." Here, too, an excavated columbarium, looking for all the world like an inverted bee-hive, serves for a ready-made tool-house, the empty cells making excellent receptacles. It is to be hoped the former patrician occupants of these diverted sepulchres did not have the same objection to the removal of their ashes as Shakespeare, otherwise the curse might well be connected with the poisonous scorpion lying so menacingly in this morning's blast.

I cannot refrain from mentioning the absorbing interest attached to this place in the minds of my friendly companions, and which afterwards cast a spell over me by its eerie reality. A hundred generations ago, came the word of Jeremiah the prophet, foretelling that, in days yet to come, Jerusalem should be rebuilt for the last time and forever, and "the city shall be built from the tower of Hananeel unto the gate of the corner. And the measuring line shall yet go forth over against it upon the hill Gareb, and shall compass about Goath." Now this is just what has happened: the building reaches straight out to the place where I am standing, there it stops, and the red-roofed houses follow a line down to the dry Kidron and the Valley of Dead Bodies, as predicted. The ashes of the old sacrifices were commanded to be buried in a clean place, and the amount consumed by the Temple offerings would in time have been great enough to form the hill; indeed, a sample has been analyzed, and found to be the ashes of animals. Only a few years ago, the remains of a tower were discovered near the Jaffa Gate which was identified as the one Hananel built in the field of Anathoth, for which seventeen shekels of silver were weighed out in the balances, and for which, to-day, 4,000 must be handed out in the rather more convenient form of Bank of England notes. I felt as if the weary and forlorn Israelites might be granted some of the prophetic promises, instead of the curses which we are rather apt to look upon as their due.

This elaborate system of proselytism is naturally costly; but the results show a grateful perception on the part of the converts, of the benefits of the combined effects of civilization and Christianity, for while the work provided to destitute Jews in Abraham's vineyard and the financial aid given them in other directions is designed, first of all, to advance their material prosperity, the hope always is present that this pure, true love and unselfishness will bear testimony to the sweet charities of a Christian life, and the shrewd Jew will contrast the squalid condition of his surroundings and his beliefs with that of his Gentile brethren, to the latter's advantage.

The estate we are leaving is designed to serve in time for a hundred Hebrew houses, but while funds are being collected, the Jews themselves do more than stand and wait. They are laborers in the field, the dressers of the vines, make the real olive soap sent to Marseilles; and it is only at the Wailing-Place on Fridays that their mild and gentle faces change to an expression, half rapture, half scowl, while their woes of the kind that are not voiceless reach the curious visitor who ventures to ask for one of the nails driven in the Temple wall to register a vow. A silver piastre will purchase the rusty bit of iron, and keep them quiet for five minutes.

This languid land of Goath has very few visitors, and the real practical hard work of the missionaries, who are guardians, helpers, and priests of the sons of Abraham, receives little praise; but it is all the more interesting for being so rarely seen, and very regretfully we climb in the saddle again, for it is difficult to believe it can hold together in the wild scamper insisted on by the donkeys, once their noses are pointed homewards. How wonderfully picturesque and beautiful is this returning! The wild-flowers at our feet are a month's study, and so are the endless views of Mizpeh and Moab, and the face of Olivet, with the towers of a hundred convents glinting in the sunshine. It is too grand to describe by fragments, more beautiful to my mind than anything I have ever seen. Soon shines out, above the roof-tops, the wonderful blue-tiled minutiæ which constitute the dome of the Harem

Esh-Shereef, — the noble Mohammedan sanctuary, built on the sacred temple site, where the ancient chroniclers relate that the Jewish Solomon with outspread hands uttered his prophetic litany: "For the strangers who are not of Thy people Israel," but, like ourselves, "come out of a far country."

www.ingramcontent.com/pod-product-compliance
Lightning Source LLC
Chambersburg PA
CBHW020800230426
43666CB00007B/784